# Sec   ls

**Extraordinary v                                    inations**

# Secret Hotels

### Extraordinary values in the world's most stunning destinations

By Erik Torkells & the editors of
*Budget Travel*

Stewart, Tabori & Chang
New York

# What's a Secret Hotel?

Too many people believe that you have to be rich to visit the world's most alluring destinations. But they're wrong.

When I became editor of *Budget Travel* in 2003, I was certain that the magazine could corner the market on what I thought of as Secret Hotels. I meant the kind of properties that don't show up on big online booking engines, or get written about in fussy travel magazines—the kind of hotels you hear about from your friends.

Our first Secret Hotels feature was on Provence, and one look at the pictures (stone farmhouses, flaky croissants, lots of smiling owners) proved what we already knew:

Keeping an eye on value doesn't have to mean cutting corners. We went on to assign more Secret Hotels stories, the best of which have been expanded into this book.

The truth is, every gorgeous destination has people who want to live there, and they open a hotel in order to make a living. They put their hearts and souls into it, doing everything they can to make certain that their guests receive the warmest welcome.

And that's why Secret Hotels are the sweetest kind of hotels. They're run by real people for real people, and they're run with love. Even if they're secrets no more.

—Erik Torkells

Right: Bali's Nirarta Centre.
Previous pages: Costa Rica's Hotel Milarepa.

# Provence

Ah, Provence. . . . The word itself is utterly relaxing, a contented sigh calling to mind bright blue skies, tall sunflowers, and quirky village markets. Popular culture has done its part to burnish the region's image—from Peter Mayle's oeuvre to Russell Crowe in *A Good Year*. Happily, Provence has no trouble living up to its reputation, and even surpassing it. And that's probably because culture, for all its power, is limited in how much it can truly appeal to your senses. Any photograph will show the beauty of Provence, but only by visiting can you smell the thyme in the air, or taste the freshly baked baguettes from the village *boulangerie*.

# Le Mas du Loriot

Chirping cicadas and rustling leaves are the only ambient noises at this quiet haven in the hills between Gordes and Roussillon in the heart of the Luberon Regional Nature Park, an area best known for its ancient villages, castles, and products such as goat cheese, honey, wine, and truffles. The hotel is on the southern slopes of the Monts de Vaucluse. Each room has a private terrace with a magnificent view: a small lavender field, and far behind it the mighty massif of the Luberon. A pool is tucked among the pine trees.

The graceful decor includes tile floors, white walls, and simple white wooden dressers and side tables. The padded headboards hang from decorative rods affixed to the wall, and their rich fabrics match the drapes. Paintings and sconces give the rooms a polished and inviting feel, and modern amenities—televisions, telephones, hairdryers, and minibars—add to the comfort. Private bathrooms are stocked with nice goodies from Yves Rocher. There's an air of privacy not found at most Provençal inns, as rooms are accessible from the outside; mingling with your neighbors is strictly voluntary.

The restaurant has a set-menu Mediterranean dinner on weekdays, which is served either on the terrace or in the dining room by the fire. Though it's not obligatory, half board is strongly encouraged—and probably not a bad idea, considering how difficult it might be to find the energy necessary to get up from your deck chair and drive into town.

If you are motivated to go out and explore the area, there are markets almost every day in Apt, Carpentras, St-Rémy-de-Provence, and Coustellet that sell crafts and produce from the local provinces. A bric-a-brac fair is held on weekends in L'Isle-sur-la-Sorgue, 30 minutes away. The hotel can also help locate outfitters to arrange walking and cycling trips from Ventoux to Luberon.
ⓘ *Murs-en-Provence, 011-33/4-90-72-62-62, masduloriot.com, $63–$157.*

**Left: The shaded pool at Le Mas du Loriot. Right: Watching over a hallway. Previous pages: Breakfast alfresco at Le Mas du Loriot**

# La Bégude Saint-Pierre

American-style amenities are rare in French hotels, but this country inn does what it can: Rooms are spacious, beds are large (two small twins clamped together); bathrooms are stocked with toiletries; and there's a sauna, a pool, and a small gym. And then there's the French part: glorious countryside views, 17th-century stone buildings with white shutters, exposed beams, and a gourmet restaurant.

**The 35 acres of grounds stretch to the Gardon River, which runs under the Pont-du-Gard**

The inside of this old postal-relay-station-turned-farm-house-turned-inn has been almost entirely reconstructed to create no-nonsense modern, air-conditioned rooms with faux antiques and Provençal bedspreads. The hotel is on a small country highway, so a few of the 23 rooms get some road noise during the daytime (even though they're quite large, the three that face the road are in the lowest price category). The south-facing rooms are filled with natural light and have views of the countryside and the swimming pool.

The 35 acres of grounds stretch to the Gardon River, which runs under the

neighboring Pont-du-Gard, an amazing chunk of still-intact Roman aqueduct designed to carry water 30 miles from the springs near Uzès to Nîmes. Listed as a UNESCO World Heritage site since 1985, the three-level aqueduct is only a 20-minute walk away—or you can borrow one of the hotel's four bicycles, available to guests free of charge.

In fact, La Bégude Saint-Pierre makes a great home base from which to explore Avignon and Nîmes, the mountains and the sea. If you really want to survey the countryside in all its glory, the hotel can help arrange a hot-air balloon excursion or a horseback ride. On Saturday, visit the daylong market in Uzès for delicious picnic supplies such as olives, cheese, and jam. ❶ *Vers-Pont-du-Gard, 011-33/4-66-63-63-63, hotel-saintpierre.fr, $88–$251.*

Right: La Bégude Saint-Pierre's backyard. Left: A guest bath. Following pages: The rustic sophistication of La Bégude Saint-Pierre

# Hôtel de l'Amphithéâtre

Style, comfort, and reasonable prices combine to make these chic lodgings a truly excellent deal. Its central location in the heart of Arles—right by the amphitheater and a short walk to the main town square and several restaurants, cafés, and bars—make it a convenient choice as well. It is also close to the Saturday market, a reliably lively affair where vendors sell everything from table linens to dried flowers to over 25 varieties of local olives.

> The Belvedere room, which has a 360-degree view of the rooftops of Arles, is worth a splurge

The owners completely renovated the building, exposing amazing 17th-century wood-beam ceilings. Wall colors tend toward rich shades of yellow, ocher, and red, and they're generally balanced with bright fabrics, regionally made quilts, light floor tiles, and modern furniture that borrows from antique styles. The cheapest rooms are on the smaller side; it's definitely worth paying the extra $12 for a "comfort" double. The Belvedere ($188), which has a 360-degree view of the rooftops of Arles, is worth a splurge. All of the rooms feature air-conditioning, there's free Wi-Fi access, and a massage therapist is on call. An outdoor terrace and an inviting lounge add to the homey feel.

Arles has much to recommend it as a destination. Vincent Van Gogh lived here in 1888, during which time he developed his signature style of vivid colors and swirling brushstrokes. It was also in Arles that he cut off his ear after quarreling with Paul Gauguin. Take a self-guided tour of the nearby locations Van Gogh represented in his paintings; they're marked with plaques. For more ambitious types, the beach in Van Gogh's *Fishing Boats on the Beach at Saintes-Maries* is less than an hour away by car. And when you've had your fill of Van Gogh, the Musée de l'Arles et de la Provence Antiques is a 15-minute walk from the hotel. ❶ *Arles, 011-33/4-90-96-10-30, hotel amphitheatre.fr, $62–$188.*

**Right: Outside Hôtel de l'Amphithéâtre. Left: The Belvedere room's door. Following pages: The hotel's sitting room, and its owners**

# Le Cadran Solaire

Once a postal-relay inn, this old stone building in the residential part of a very small town has thick walls, a tranquil atmosphere (reinforced by the absence of televisions in the rooms), and a trellised garden. It's named for the sundial found on the front of the building that dates back to 1846. With high-beamed ceilings and garden views, the 12 rooms are luminous; ornate modern bedsteads, period reproduction furniture, and muted colors complete the decor. The friendly owners live on the premises and try to make the place feel like a private home, and by and large they succeed. Homemade orange, apricot, and raspberry marmalades accompany breakfast on the terrace or in the dining room.

**The friendly owners live on the premises and try to make Le Cadran Solaire feel like a private home**

Though not neighboring any major tourist sites, Graveson is five miles north of St-Rémy-de-Provence and within a half-hour drive of most Provençal highlights. Then again, the town itself has a relaxed southern charm—which might be more what you're looking for in Provence, anyway.

Huge plane trees shade a tiny canal that cuts across the main square, and

from May to October there's a Friday market where cheese and produce are sold. A walk along the town's streets will take you past the 12th-century Notre Dame du Bon Remède chapel, the fortified door of the Romanesque church, the 17th-century Breuil château, and Saint Michel de Frigolet church.

When they're not attending church services, the residents might be making *santons* (handcrafted figurines that resemble real people) or candles. There are also two museums visitors will find worth investigating: the Musée des Arômes et du Parfum, which has exhibits on the region's 1,000-year-old tradition of perfumery and aromatherapy, and the museum dedicated to 20th-century Provençal painter Auguste Chabaud. ⓘ *Graveson, 011-33/4-90-95-71-79, hotel-en-provence.com, $75–$103.*

Right: A fresh start at Le Cadran Solaire. Left: A guest bath. Following pages: Inside, and out, at Le Cadran Solaire

# Hôtel de l'Atelier

Spare yourself the agony of trying to find high-season lodgings in Avignon—there's a great little hotel across the river in Villeneuve, a charming medieval village just a five-minute bus ride from the City of Popes.

The building was constructed in the 16th century as a silk workshop, and the 23 rooms are all different shapes and sizes. There are exposed beams and stone walls, as well as painted niches, Art Deco dressers, Chinese end tables, and antique photography. (Something about a few of the rooms brings to mind a 1940s movie set.) A stone stairway, bathed in light, creates the feeling of an interior Italian courtyard. The garden terrace is livened up with modern sculpture, and hallways showcase paintings by local artists. An old fireplace

in the living room adds character and is a great place to curl up with a cup of tea.

Villeneuve hosts a traditional market (with vendors selling fruit, flowers, and fish) on Thursdays and Saturdays; there's also an antiques market on Saturday mornings. On non-market days visitors should check out Philippe le Bel Tower for panoramas of the Rhone valley, then wander over to the Pierre de Luxembourg museum (home to 16th- and 17th-century regional art) and Fort Saint André (which once protected the town). When it's time for wine-tasting, there are wineries such as Lirac and Saint Laurent des Arbres. ❶ *Villeneuve-lez-Avignon, 011-33/4-90-25-01-84, hotel delatelier.com, $67–$131.*

**Right: Inside Hôtel de l'Atelier. Left: Looking down at the garden. Following pages: Sun-drenched Hôtel de l'Atelier**

# Auberge du Presbytère

The old stone presbytery, with foundations dating back to the 11th and 12th centuries, dominates La Place de la Fontaine, the tiny main square of Saignon, in the Luberon region. This is a beautiful eagle's nest of a village (one of the 10 oldest in France) that peers down on a valley and the town of Apt, three miles away. The Auberge was in the same hands—an American expat's—for a long time, as you can tell from the lived-in, un-hotel-like ambience that the new German owner is dedicated to preserving.

> **Rooms are tastefully decorated with Provençal prints and paintings by the former owner's wife**

Rooms are tastefully decorated with a variety of rattan armchairs, throw rugs, local antiques, Provençal prints, and interesting paintings by the former owner's wife. Two rooms have incredible views, one with a 270-degree panorama of the Luberon massif with the 12th-century village church in the foreground. As one would expect, the smaller rooms are cheaper; the least expensive is cute but really tiny, with a bathroom in the hall.

The hotel's restaurant is a good bet—and not just because any alternatives are a long haul down the hill (and, even worse, back up again afterward). Lamb from Luberon is regularly featured on the menu. Reservations are essential, as the restaurant is small and popular.

On Saturday mornings there's a market in Apt. Other highlights of Saignon include the 900-year-old *bories* (stone huts), cobbled Roman paths, and Notre Dame de Pitié church located in front of city hall. It's an easy hike to the summit of Saignon, which, on a clear day, offers gorgeous views of the Luberon region and the Alps of High Provence. Other neighboring sights include a museum in Ménerbes devoted to corkscrews and a museum in Bonnieux that's devoted to bread. ❶ *Saignon, 011-33/4-90-74-11-50, auberge-presbytere.com, $73–$185 (closed mid-January to mid-February).*

Left: The inviting exterior of Auberge du Presbytère. Right: *Fromage* at the hotel's restaurant. Following pages: A guest room at Auberge du Presbytère, and its owners

# L'Hôtel Sous les Figuiers

The name means "hotel under the fig trees," and sure enough, Sous les Figuiers boasts 13 rooms that each have a terrace and a small private yard with a fig tree that you can harvest at will (the three that don't have trees cost at least $12 less). Somewhere between a B&B and a hotel, this low-key lodging is on a quiet street in a residential area just a couple of minutes from the center of town.

> If you like the faux finish on the armoire, you can learn how to do it yourself at one of the art workshops

The hotel reopened in 2003 after a change in ownership and a complete renovation. The place is spick-and-span, from the lushly painted walls to the earth-toned tiles in the bathrooms. The entryway to the rooms is filled with antique furniture, flowers, and the owner's artwork, and is lit with large candle-lanterns at night. The modern rooms are softened with quilted bedcovers and restored antiques. There's a cheerful breakfast room where only fresh, local products are served; the bread comes directly from the town's bakery each morning.

The friendly owner encourages guests to get to know each other over a game of chess or an evening aperitif, but you can also just lounge by the pool on your own or stretch out under your fig tree and take a nap.

The hotel has an art studio where individual and group classes are offered in *trompe l'oeil*, patinas, and frescoes—so if you like the faux finish on the armoire, you can learn how to do it yourself. For those less inclined to dirty their hands, local galleries feature the work of more than 100 area painters and sculptors.

St-Rémy-de-Provence is within the protected area of the Alpilles, where vineyards and orchards sit adjacent to wildlife areas. (For all its sophistication, Provence is also home to wild boars, Egyptian vultures, and the rare Bonelli's eagle.) Hiking, horseback riding, and bicycling are just a few of the possible activities. ➊ *St-Rémy-de-Provence, 011-33/4-32-60-15-40, hotel-charme-provence.com, $107–$145.*

**Right:** The owner's artwork at L'Hôtel Sous les Figuiers. **Left:** The inn's breakfast room

Potiron
9,50 €/kg

# Bali

The Indonesian island of Bali is one of those places that people return from changed—they look at the world differently, more gratefully. In a purely physical sense, Bali is blessed with a dual nature: It's simultaneously spectacular and soothing, with dramatic mountains and valleys tempered by babbling streams and gently rustling leaves. But that's not what makes the biggest impression on its visitors. Simply put, Bali is home to the nicest people on the planet. They take nothing for granted—not their beautiful island, not their good fortune to live there, and certainly not their guests, whom they treat with love and respect.

# Nirarta Centre for Living Awareness

One of the things that first attracted Western visitors to Bali at the beginning of the 20th century was its rich spiritual tradition, which draws on elements of Hinduism, Buddhism, and animism and recognizes the importance of the balanced coexistence of the individual and the wider world. These days, most visitors pursue physical pleasures, but anyone interested in exploring the inner self might like the Nirarta Centre.

Founded by British psychologist Peter Wrycza and his Balinese wife, Dayu Mayuni, Nirarta Centre has 11 rooms total in six cottages, some of which have two stories. Built of wood and stone with grass or shingle roofs, the spacious cottages—two are octagonal, from a traditional Hindu symbol—are simple but comfortable and offer pretty valley views. The center sits amid rice terraces and has its own extensive vegetable gardens, which supply most of the largely vegetarian food served in a separate, open-sided restaurant.

Nirarta offers a number of coaching and counseling courses. Guests are free to take part in two daily 45-minute meditation sessions, which are held in the large meditation hall (also octagonal). Guided visits to traditional healers, sacred sites, hidden temples, energy spots, weavers, farmers, and local families can also be arranged by the staff. Although the focus is on spiritual and cultural activities, the physical is not entirely overlooked; close to the river there's a small massage center with just one massage table. The river itself is what the hotel cheekily calls its "natural Jacuzzi." ⓘ *Sidemen, 011-62/366-24-122, awareness-bali.com, from $30, fees for non-meditation courses.*

Left: A soothing space at Nirarta. Above: A spiritual detail, and the "natural Jacuzzi." Preceding pages: The grounds at Nirarta Centre

# Ulun Ubud Resort & Spa

In an open-air workshop just to the west of Ubud, the island's cultural capital, a young wood-carver is carefully contemplating his latest work—a goddess slowly emerging from a twisted tree trunk. When he's satisfied at last, he marks the wood and begins his carving again.

The craftsman's boss is Gus Tu, son of a noted local wood-carver and owner of the Ulun Ubud, which sits next to the workshop. The artistic heritage is obvi-

ous as you meander down the paths and steep steps linking the hotel's 22 thatched cottages: Every nook holds a statue or a carving—a Hindu warrior here, a head of the Buddha there, and everywhere countless carved frogs, fish, shrimps, and crabs. The rooms are simple but comfortable, decorated with traditional Balinese antiques and original paintings, and air-conditioned, with bathrooms that could do with a little updating and wide balconies that overlook a lush river valley and rice paddies.

The hotel has a reasonable restaurant serving Balinese and Western fare, and there's a free shuttle if you're feeling inclined to sample some of Ubud's many restaurants. Art galleries, shopping, and entertainment are a shuttle ride away as well. Spend a day rafting; visiting hot springs; or attending traditional theater, dance, or music performances; then return to the hotel spa for a Balinese Boreh therapy session. This 1,000-year-old cure for muscle exhaustion and pain begins with a thorough massage followed by a body mask of pepper, clove, cinnamon, and chili powder; it ends with a restorative soak in aromatic bath oil and a cup of refreshing ginger tea.

If you take breakfast on your balcony, you may hear the distant chink-chink-chink of iron on stone. Look down toward the river and you'll see that along its banks, local craftspeople are cutting stone to make new carvings, some of which may well show up on the hotel's rambling grounds. ❶ *Ubud, 011-62/361-975-024, ulunubud.com, from $75, includes breakfast.*

Left: Ulun Ubud's open-air living area. Right: A mosaic floor. Following pages: A room at Ulun Ubud, and a view of the grounds

# Nirvana Pension & Gallery

I Nyoman Suradnya is a little concerned about the state of tourism in Bali: "The relation between Balinese and tourists is too much business," says the artist. At their homestay, located just off the main street in the center of Ubud, Suradnya and his wife, Ni Wayan Rai Rupini, who owns several jewelry and crafts shops, are trying to turn tourists into guests by opening their home and allowing visitors to observe day-to-day Balinese life as well as traditional rituals.

In their family compound, which Suradnya designed, it's hard to say where the home ends and the hotel begins—reflecting, in good part, Suradnya's strong belief in maintaining the three harmonies essential for a human: harmony with one's god, harmony with other humans, and harmony with the natural world. The rooms blend seamlessly with a stone shrine and Suradnya's open-sided studio. Plants, trees, and songbirds pepper the grounds. There are just four rooms in the homestay ("I want to leave time for my art," explains Suradnya), in two small pavilions. Each room has attractive paintings in bold reds, greens, and golds on wood; its own bathroom; and a peaceful balcony or terrace.

*For many guests, the real attraction at Nirvana is Suradnya, who specializes in teaching batik*

For many guests, the real attraction is Suradnya. While he's a gifted painter, he specializes in teaching batik, a traditional Indonesian method of patterning fabric using wax and dyes. Batik classes lasting from one day ($35) to five days ($125) are offered three days a week. Suradnya describes the processes involved as "meditation in action"—a way to focus on what you're doing in the here and now. Guests are also invited to learn the significance and importance of daily offerings and how to craft them from colored cakes and carved leaves ($20 per person). As Suradnya speaks, his granddaughter jumps up behind him and rings a bell. "We ring that bell to call people to lunch," he says with a grin. "It's how we invite them to come back to the present." ❶ *Ubud, 011-62/361-975-415, nirvanaku.com, from $22.*

Left: Nirvana's owner, I Nyoman Suradnya, with his granddaughter. Right: One of the rooms. Following pages: Carved doors leading to a Nirvana guest room

# Puri Lumbung Cottages

The village of Munduk is a world away from the beaches that draw most tourists to Bali. Life here moves at a different pace: Farmers lay out cloves and cocoa beans along the road to dry in the sun, village dogs meander about, and the sound of chanting drifts in on the evening breeze.

To introduce visitors to his world, I Nyoman Bagiarta set up the Puri Lumbung Cottages in a garden bursting with guava, lime, papaya, pineapple, and other tropical fruits. Modeled after the human form, the property has a shrine at the head, accommodations at the heart, and other facilities at the foot. In 12 of the 17 cottages, the top floor was converted from an old *lumbung*—a rice granary of wood and bamboo, with a thatched roof (Bagiarta has chosen to substitute shingles). Behind intricately carved doors there's room for a bed with a woven headboard, a blue quilt picturing local flora or fauna, a mosquito net suspended from the underside of the peaked roof, and not much more. Open slatted areas above the doors and screenless shuttered windows let in the air. There's also a balcony and a bathroom on the lower floor, so the cottages don't feel cramped.

> Modeled after the human form, Puri Lumbung has a shrine at the head and guest rooms at the heart

The hotel doesn't have a pool, but there's still plenty to do, including trekking, listening to live gamelan music, participating in traditional Balinese dance classes, walking to a secret waterfall, and taking part in a local reforestation project. In the evening, you can dine in the hotel's restaurant, which serves traditional Balinese and Indonesian dishes, including *timbungan be siap* (a chicken soup with cassava leaves and shallots), and offers great views of the surrounding hills. Guests marvel again and again at the beautiful sunsets over the rice fields and the coast.

Bagiarta is a charming host, but he wants to do more than just cater to visitors. He believes that people, not the hotel, are the attraction and that he can help his community by bringing in jobs and acting as a template for other hotels owned and run by Balinese. He's succeeded: The hotel has already inspired a number of locals to open their own homestays. "If people copy, OK," he says with a smile. ℹ *Munduk, 011-62/362-92-810, purilumbung.com, from $75.*

**Right: A rustic cottage at Puri Lumbung. Left: A handmade latch in one of the rooms**

# Rumah Cantik

In northern Bali, Lovina is a miniature version of the hugely popular resort towns that lie along the island's south coast. So it might seem surprising that just 200 yards or so from the area's main drag is a place of peace and quiet.

The Rumah Cantik—a homestay with four rooms in a flower-filled tropical garden—was built by Made Kantra and Jette Stampe, a Balinese-Danish couple, and its eclectic design reflects its owners' backgrounds. On the outside of the two pavilions housing the guest rooms, European-style pillars support a Balinese roof with upturned eaves. Inside, the mix of influences continues in the generous guest rooms: The four-poster king-size beds are done up with white canopies, while the other furniture, made by traditional Balinese craftsmen, has a hint of Japanese simplicity. Cushions and pillows circle a low table to form a sitting area, and carved masks and other art decorate the walls. The large bathrooms have floors and walls made of layers of gray stones.

In the garden, the feel is Balinese, with a large *bale*, or open-sided living room, surrounded by a small fish pond. On sunny afternoons, reflections from the water dance on the *bale*'s ceiling. There isn't a lot to do, and that's deliberate: no pool, no TV, and—apart from breakfast and light snacks—no restaurant. Then again, doing nothing may be exactly what you crave. When hunger strikes, there are plenty of restaurants within walking distance, and a visit to Batur Volcano or a dolphin safari off Lovina Beach is just a short ride away. Wi-Fi connections are provided in all rooms. Rumah Cantik can be hard to find; if you tend to have difficulty navigating, Kantra and Stampe will meet you on the main road. ❶ *Lovina, 011-62/362-42-159, lovinacantik.com, from $65.*

Left: One of the four guest rooms at Rumah Cantik homestay. Right: The house proper, and looking out to a patio

# Blue Moon Villas

Though it's long been popular with adventurous divers and snorkelers, Bali's remote northeast coast, an area of small fishing villages, is still well off the beaten track for most visitors to the island. That may change if more hotels follow the example of Blue Moon Villas, a stylish little boutique hotel that makes the most of its dramatic coastal setting.

Designed by local architect Pak Jaya, the hotel has five rooms in three bright, airy villas, as well as an open-sided lobby/restaurant. The rooms have white walls and are simply furnished. Hot pink and turquoise iridescent silk pillows and throws add cheery accents. All rooms have separate dressing areas and balconies or terraces, some of which are large enough to double as living rooms. As in many Balinese hotels, the bathrooms are partly open to the outside (but completely private).

The staff is friendly but less deferential than in the main Balinese resorts—which could be because many of the staff members are related to the hotel's co-owner, Komang John, an engaging local guy who also gave his name to the hotel's restaurant. After a dinner of fresh wahoo barbecued over coconut husks, you'll want to sit on your balcony and watch the fishing boats fan out

into the ocean. Stay to see the sun set behind the sacred mountain Agung, a prelude to the main event: the brilliant night sky. In the wee hours it's not unusual to catch a shooting star.

If the local roosters wake you up in time, you can go out in a fishing boat in the morning to watch the sun rise over Mount Rinjani on the neighboring island of Lombok, and maybe spot a dolphin or a flying fish. Late risers can still take in the expansive view of the horizon over the ocean from a small infinity pool tucked in the center of a lush garden filled with bougainvilleas, hibiscuses, and gardenias. ⓘ *Amed, 011-62/812-362-2597, bluemoonvillas.com, from $60.*

Right: The garden path at Blue Moon Villas. Left: The pool. Following pages: Sunny days (and sunny dispositions) at Blue Moon

# Patal Kikian

In 1963, Ida Ayu Mas Andayani and her family fled their home when Mount Agung erupted. "Stones and rocks fell from the sky," recalls Andayani. The eruption was Agung's first in 120 years, and while the mountain has been quiet ever since, experts warn that it may indeed erupt again. Andayani is certain to cope with whatever nature throws her way; she's not the kind of woman to be put off for long by a mere volcano. The descendant of an important local family and wife of the chief of culture of Sidemen, she has welcomed an impressive list of guests to her intimate homestay, from Indonesian presidents to international artists and musicians, including the likes of Mick Jagger, David Bowie, and Roman Polanski.

> Past guests at Patal Kikian include the likes of Mick Jagger and David Bowie

Andayani began building the three well-spaced villas in 1979, although they look as if they've been around for centuries. The villas are red brick and gray stone, and covered in intricately carved panels depicting scenes from Hindu epics. Fanned by breezes, the villas' wide terraces make for cool and

calm outdoor living rooms with broad views of the volcano, rice terraces, and the lush river valley. Among the flowers in Patal Kikian's pretty gardens are fruit trees—papaya, durian, avocado, rambutan, and more—that supply just-picked produce for guests' meals. Inside, the bathrooms are a bit functional-looking, but the bedrooms are large and tastefully furnished with antiques and original paintings, many by Andayani's friends.

And Andayani is just the person to ask if you're interested in learning more about the area's rich cultural heritage. She can arrange for guests to visit weavers—making the traditional hand-loomed fabrics Bali is known for, ikat and gold-brocaded *songket*—in their homes in Sidemen, a 25-minute walk away. The village temple is especially festive on ceremony days, when the gamelan orchestra performs; Andayani knows the calendar. ⓘ *Sidemen, 011-62/366-23-005, patalkikian@gmail.com, from $45 (includes breakfast) or $65 (includes three meals a day).*

**Right:** A quiet path at Patal Kikian. **Left:** Inside one of the three guest villas

# Cornwall

Even the English like to hang loose now and again, and when they're in the mood they head to Cornwall. The peninsula, on England's southwest tip, is where the country's surf culture sprouted up, and it retains that down-to-earth vibe. (In fact, it may be the only place in England where the word *vibe* won't draw a titter.) Visitors to the Cornish coast soak up the sun, take a dip in the Atlantic, tour the many famous gardens, or simply hang out on the lawn with a good book. And as might be expected, the seafood is superb. Cornwall is an ideal respite from foggy London—especially, it seems, if you happen to be a celebrity chef.

# Old Coastguard Hotel

As its name implies, the Old Coastguard Hotel is a former lookout for the Coast Guard. Consequently, it has the best ocean views in the harbor town of Mousehole (pronounced *mau*-zel), which Dylan Thomas called "the most beautiful village in England." Picture windows look out on the bay in many rooms, which are decorated simply in a contemporary style, with beech and pine furniture and beige and brown fabrics. Of the 23 rooms, eight are in the Lodge, a newer annex down the hill.

**Guests bask on the sunbaked rocks, while children investigate the natural tide pools, fishnets at the ready**

At the hotel's award-winning restaurant, the catch of the day (brought straight to the kitchen from the fish market at nearby Newlyn Harbour) is jazzed up with Thai spices, tangy salsas, and saffron. Lobsters are fresh from small boats right in Mousehole Harbor.

Not far from Land's End, the western-most point in mainland England,

Mousehole is a wonderfully typical English fishing village—and an old one: Part of its south quay dates from the 14th century. The little cove is surrounded by cute shops, pubs, and tearooms. It's easy to lose an afternoon exploring the ones that seem appealing.

A walkway traces the coastline from the harbor and passes by the stone steps that lead up to the Old Coastguard Hotel's back garden gate. When the tide is out, boulders are revealed just below the path. Guests love to bask on the sunbaked rocks, while children investigate the natural tide pools, their long-handled fishnets at the ready. ❶ *Mousehole, 011-44/173-673-1222, oldcoastguardhotel.co.uk, from $158, includes breakfast.*

Right: The dining room at Old Coastguard. Left: A guest room. Previous pages: The view from Old Coastguard's patio

## ST. IVES
# Primrose Valley Hotel

Outside the front door lies a jumble of buckets and spades, wet suits in a rainbow of colors, and children's neoprene swimming socks. Just inside, a window ledge is crowded with wedding portraits, baby pictures, and some shots of then-shaggy-haired owners Andrew and Sue Biss taken in the early '90s. "We're slightly embarrassed of those," Andrew says. He needn't be: Primrose Valley is the kind of family-friendly place that lets it all hang out—and stylishly so.

Since buying the Edwardian villa in 2001, the Bisses have ripped up old carpet to reveal hardwood floors, and they've nixed heavy antiques in favor of contemporary oak tables and soft Italian leather chairs. In the full-service bar and kitchen, the Bisses and Sue's mother, Rose, whip up full English breakfasts and picnic lunches for those who request them. Providing sustainable tourism and supporting local suppliers are the inn's credos, from the beef (steaks from the only family butcher that still owns its own grazing fields) to the bath soap (avocado and tea-tree oil produced by a local mother-daughter team).

The 10 bedrooms come with private baths and vary in size. Four have ocean views—two from covered balconies. A new modern suite is a recent addition, sporting a red leather couch and a sleek bedroom, complete with a flat-screen television. Primrose Valley is located on a residential cul-de-sac just across a set of raised railroad tracks from crescent-shaped Porthminster Beach, and four other beautiful beaches are nearby. As the hotel's website says, it's "bed to beach in under a minute."

The quaint town is home to galleries, studios, and even an outpost of London's world-renowned Tate collections

Surfing is a popular pastime in the area, and dolphins and seals can often be spotted in the bay. The nearby town of St. Ives, a five-minute walk, has been an artists' enclave since the 19th century. (J.M.W. Turner, James McNeill Whistler, and Barbara Hepworth all lived in St. Ives at one time or another.) Its narrow cobblestone streets are home to galleries, studios, and even an outpost of London's world-renowned Tate collections. ❶ *St. Ives, 011-44/173-679-4939, primroseonline.co.uk, from $140, includes breakfast.*

**Clockwise from top left:**
**The beach outside Primrose**
**Valley Hotel, the front patio,**
**a seat by the sea, the owners.**
**Right: Family mementos**

# Trehellas House

Built in 1740, Trehellas House was originally an inn. It was converted to a farmhouse in the late 1800s and a private home in the 20th century—it even served as a courthouse for a short time. Some of its history is evident in the courtroom suite, where there's a cut-glass chandelier, a wood-burning fireplace, and a large bed that rests on what was formerly the judge's dais. (Another remnant of the past is the friendly resident ghost, Mr. Lobb, a farmer who owned Trehellas House around 200 years ago.)

> The friendly resident ghost, Mr. Lobb, was a farmer who owned Trehellas House around 200 years ago

The 10 other rooms have a comfortable country feel, with patchwork quilts, floral curtains, and iron beds. They're scattered throughout the main building and in a coach house annex across the gravel driveway. The restaurant, in one of the oldest and most striking parts of the building, still has the original slate floor, low-beamed ceilings, and a fireplace that's lit on cold nights. The work of local Cornish photographers and artists decorates the walls.

The hotel grounds are planted with an array of soft grasses, flowering shrubs, and heathers. A sunken stone patio surrounded by a stone wall is dotted with deck chairs and potted plants. Most notably, there's a large heated

swimming pool—it's an unusual feature for such an historic English inn.

Trehellas House is a wonderful base for those inclined to investigate Cornwall's many garden tours. The property backs right onto the Pencarrow estate, a Georgian home with 50 acres to explore. Also nearby is Lanhydrock House, with extensive gardens of its own and a kitchen that would make the likes of Martha Stewart swoon (or perhaps even try to buy the place): There are separate larders for fish and meat and a marble-countered dairy to keep puddings cool. The hugely popular Eden Project—home to two enormous biomes that contain plants from all around the globe—is a quick 15-minute drive away. ⓘ *Bodmin, 011-44/120-872-700, trehellashouse. co.uk, from $136, includes breakfast.*

**Right: Trehellas House's backyard. Left: One of the 11 rooms. Following pages: Trehellas House, overflowing with greenery**

# Trevalsa Court Country House Hotel

German expats Klaus Wagner and Matthias Mainka have devoted the last seven years creating a sumptuous pre–World War II atmosphere at Trevalsa Court Country House Hotel, formerly a family home that dates from 1937. They've obsessed over every detail, right down to the door handles.

The 13 rooms are furnished with Lloyd Loom woven chairs, and the moss-green walls are decorated with sophisticated black-and-white art. In the main sitting room, afternoon light streams through mullioned windows, lemons are piled elegantly in a silver bowl, roses float in a shallow vase, and glossy art books—in English, German, and French—are stacked on the coffee tables. The level of care is palpable.

> Light streams through mullioned windows, lemons are piled elegantly in a silver bowl, and roses float in a shallow vase

As it should be, dinner is served in the oak-paneled dining room, where tables are set with candles and white tablecloths, and windows frame the sea. The German chef, Achim Dreher, sneaks Swiss-German influences into his menus. Guests will want to keep an eye open for highlights such as apple strudel and potato dumplings stuffed with prunes.

Wagner and Mainka planted the garden with spiky palms, camellias, and

flowering bulbs that bloom at different times of the year. "It definitely looks like a Cornish seaside garden," says Wagner. "But we also have palm trees and other things to remind you that you're on holiday." It's a pleasant place to spend a morning: Several pairs of Adirondack chairs on the lawn face out to the sea.

A path at the end of the garden leads to secluded, and highly swimmable, Polstreath Beach. A different footpath leads to the harbor and the typically Cornish town of Mevagissey. For those willing to trek just a little farther, the Lost Gardens of Heligan—a massive garden restoration project—are two miles away. *ⓘ Mevagissey, 011-44/172-684-2468, trevalsa-hotel.co.uk, from $158, includes breakfast.*

*Right: A Trevalsa sitting room. Left: Owners Mainka and Wagner. Following pages: A taste of the good life at Trevalsa Court*

# Mill House Inn

In a small wooded valley between two fishing villages, at the bottom of a steep road, this 18th-century former corn mill looks higgledy-piggledy, with roofs and windows at all different levels. A young crowd passes the time on slouchy sofas in the reception area, waitresses crack jokes with the patrons ("If you don't eat that garnish, we'll use it again for your main course"), and a few friendly dogs lie at their masters' feet on the bar's original flagstone floor.

Visitors feel less like hotel guests than locals who've popped down to the pub for a pint. Make that gastropub: The restaurant attracts diners from around Cornwall with locally sourced seafood and meats. Weather permitting, drinks are served outside on the split-level terrace, also the site of delightful weekly barbecues with live music. On chilly evenings, a fire creates a warm, cozy atmosphere in the dining room.

Upstairs in the nine bedrooms, meanwhile, the owners have gone for a rustic-minimalist look. The thick, whitewashed stone walls are unadorned, setting off the dark wood of the headboards and desks. All of the rooms have pretty views of the Mill House's gardens; from No. 6 and No. 9, you can just spy the sea—on a clear day, anyway. The village of Tintagel, three miles from the inn, is home to the remains of a castle said to have been owned by King Arthur, and Trebarwith Strand Beach is a half mile down the road. ❶ *Trebarwith, 011-44/184-077-0200, themillhouseinn.co.uk, from $140, includes breakfast.*

> All of the rooms have pretty views of the inn's gardens; from No. 6 and No. 9 you can just spy the sea—on a clear day, anyway

Left: Hanging out at Mill House's gastropub. Above: The inn, which was a corn mill back in the 18th century

# Mount Haven Hotel

Orange Trevillion was drawn to Penzance, at the end of Cornwall, because of the town's proximity to St. Michael's Mount, an ancient craggy island that looks like a lopsided volcano. "It's a sacred place," says Trevillion, an eccentric with carrot-colored hair who believes that four of the earth's energy lines come together here. Formerly the site of a Benedictine priory and rumored to have once been home to a giant, the island got its name when a fisherman claimed to have seen the Archangel Michael there many years ago.

Trevillion and her partners bought Mount Haven in 2001 and created a friendly retreat. They knocked down walls and reconfigured the old coach house to maximize views of St. Michael's Mount and the ocean. Most of the 18 rooms look out on the water. They have an Asian feel, with silk bedspreads and throw pillows in embroidered fabrics from Trevillion's frequent trips to

India. Tapestries from Jaipur decorate the walls, and the scent of incense completes the mood. (No. 6 is the quietest, away from both the front desk and the terrace.)

Spa treatments, including reflexology, aromatherapy, and massages, are available in the Healing Room. In the restaurant, many dishes are flavored with curry and lemongrass—and even the dining room has views of the Mount from one end.

The best vistas, however, are from the terrace: You can see St. Michael's Mount rising steeply out of the water, a medieval castle perched on its tippy-top. (The castle, which is owned by the National Trust, is open to the public.) At low tide, when people stroll across a granite causeway to visit, they appear to walk on the water. Twelve miles away, beyond Mounts Bay and Penzance—the city forever associated with Gilbert and Sullivan's opera—is Land's End. ⓘ *Penzance, 011-44/173-671-0249, mount haven.co.uk, from $147, includes breakfast.*

**Right: Mount Haven's dining room. Left, from top: One of the serene rooms, and an artifact from the owner's travels**

# Rick Stein's Café

British celebrity chef Rick Stein has created a dining empire in Padstow over the last 30 years, turning a once-sleepy fishing village into a destination for foodies. "I've lived here since the 1970s and love its sense of timelessness—a little peace and tranquillity in a madly rushing world," says Stein.

The narrow, winding streets of the town radiate out from the harbor, and visitors who wander amid the shops and restaurants will inevitably find themselves outside one of Stein's many establishments: The Seafood Restaurant, St. Petroc's Bistro, Padstow Seafood School, Stein's Deli, Stein's Patisserie, Stein's Fish & Chips, and Rick Stein's Café. Dinner at the Café is the most affordable way to experience Stein's way with seafood. The menu changes seasonally and features delicious yet very accessible entrées such as whole deviled mackerel with a tomato and onion salad or deep-fried plaice with tartar sauce. Some dishes, like Thai fish cakes and grilled cod with spicy noodles, have Asian notes.

Like any good host, Stein—having fed his guests—puts them up for the night, in one of four locations around town (The Seafood Restaurant, St. Petroc's Hotel, St. Edmund's House, and Rick Stein's Café). The three rooms above the Café are snug but comfortable. Stein's wife and business partner, Jill, designed the French-accented interiors: wrought-iron beds blanketed in white *matelassé*, toile and gingham fabrics on the windows and pillows, rattan furniture, gild-framed oil paintings and mirrors, and ornamental fireplaces. Breakfast is served in the Café and features hearty fare such as bacon sandwiches on homemade bread and Parmesan-and-smoked-haddock omelettes.

Bear in mind that in high season (June, July, and August) and during school holidays Padstow can turn into a giant tourist scrum. And no matter what time of year it is, visitors should be sure to make dinner reservations well in advance in order to avoid disappointment. ⓘ *Padstow, 011-44/184-153-2700, rickstein.com, from $149, includes breakfast.*

Left: Rooms at Rick Stein's Café were decorated by Stein's wife and business partner, Jill. Right: The foyer

# Watergate Bay Hotel

The 70-room Watergate Bay Hotel is in a prime location on the cliffs above a wide, sandy beach. Over the years—and after many renovations—the Victorian hotel has morphed into a full-service resort, equal parts stylish getaway and adrenaline-filled activity center. It has become especially popular with young surfers, who come year-round from all over England.

*The second part of the complex includes a funky beach bar where reggae is almost always being played*

Recently revamped guest rooms have been transformed into modern, beach-chic havens with clean lines and blond wood furniture. Beige-on-white bedding and flat-screen televisions complete the contemporary look. The main building also houses a glass-fronted restaurant and bar, heated indoor and outdoor swimming pools, a small spa, a billiards room, squash and tennis courts, and a playroom with table tennis.

A short, sloping driveway just beyond the parking lot leads to the water's edge and to the second part of the Watergate Bay complex, which includes a funky beach bar where reggae is almost always playing. It's the perfect spot

for a casual lunch—salads, sandwiches, ice-cold beer—especially if you can snag one of the window tables with views of bobbing surfers. In summer, a grill is rolled out to the walkway next to the beach so diners can order burgers without washing the sand from their feet. A lively recent addition is Jamie "Naked Chef" Oliver's newest restaurant, Fifteen Cornwall, which showcases his innovative menu, serving the best local seasonal produce in a relaxed atmosphere with incredible views of the two-mile-long beach.

Also in the building is the Extreme Academy, which offers rentals and lessons for surfing and a bunch of sports most people have never heard of (waveskiing, kite-landboarding, traction kiting). The city of Newquay—a popular spot for destination bachelor and bachelorette parties (or stag and hen parties, as the Brits call them)—is a few minutes down the coast. Better to skip it and have a sunset drink on the terrace at Watergate Bay, or head 20 minutes north to Padstow. Anyone looking for complete relaxation should indulge in one of the 14 massages available in the hotel spa. ⓘ *Watergate Bay, 011-44/163-786-0543, watergatebay.co.uk, from $158, includes breakfast.*

Right: The terrace at Watergate Bay Hotel. Left: The restaurant. Following pages: The Watergate's backyard

# Costa Rica

Costa Rica's efforts to preserve its many natural wonders have resulted not only in making the Central American nation greener, but also in attracting like-minded souls to visit. Many of those visitors liked it so much that they decided to move there and open up accommodations. Nowhere is that more so than the southern corner of the Nicoya Peninsula: Expats from the United States, Switzerland, France, and other places have created a lively, if scattershot, community of lodgings that strive to improve their guests' experiences, while also respecting the Costa Rican land. Never has doing good *felt* so good.

# Ylang Ylang Beach Resort

It takes a certain confidence to put up a hotel that requires a 15-minute hike on the beach to get to, but Ylang Ylang pulls it off. (If you're not feeling up to the trek, you can arrange a lift for yourself and/or your bags from sister property El Sano Banano, located in town.)

Shielded from the ocean by palm trees, the resort is in a jungle clearing with 300 feet of white-sand beach bordering a wildlife preserve. Ylang Ylang's main, two-story building has six rooms, each with pale-yellow walls decorated with original watercolors of local birds. Woven blankets with colorful stripes are tucked neatly across the beds. The eight bungalows are more private; all but one have ocean views from their patios. Stone walkways connect the buildings (one is home to a beautiful yoga studio) and are lined with flowering plants and trees—including the fragrant ylang-ylang, as the hotel's name indicates.

> The restaurant's menu was created by a French chef, who returns periodically to add new dishes

The small swimming pool, which has its own waterfall, is natural-looking enough that it's no surprise that monkeys and iguanas—as well as more exotic animals, like kinkajous, agoutis, and coatis—share the lush gardens and surrounding vegetation.

The hotel restaurant's menu was created by a French chef, who came over to train the kitchen staff and now returns periodically to add new dishes such as grilled sea bass in a sauce of tomatoes, mushrooms, and basil.

Montezuma is the most compact and walkable town on the southern part of the Nicoya Peninsula. During the day, street vendors sell jewelry and beaded caps from folding tables; at night, expat surfers and tourists can be found barhopping along the bustling main drag. ❶ *Montezuma, 011-506/642-0636, elbanano.com, from $120, includes breakfast and candlelit dinner.*

Left: Ylang Ylang's pool. Right: The dining area. Preceding pages: Bungalows at Ylang Ylang

# Amor de Mar

Perched at the mouth of the Montezuma River, on a rocky point overlooking the Pacific coastline, an Adirondack-style lodge houses Amor de Mar's 11 rooms. Most are paneled in dark wood and decorated sparely (open shelves to hold your belongings and a small bar for hanging clothing), so as not to distract from the views (best from the second-floor porch). All but two rooms have private baths.

*The wide front lawn slopes toward a rocky point, where there's a tide pool big enough to swim in*

Next to the hotel are two family-friendly bungalows, Casa Luna and Casa Sol. The owners, who bought the property after coming to Montezuma on vacation in 1991, used to live in the bungalows (back then, the bungalows were connected). Both have a huge master bedroom upstairs with a balcony that has views of the garden and ocean; the first floor has a full kitchen with a refrigerator, stove, coffeemaker, and dishes.

A patio restaurant overlooking the ocean serves breakfast all day, emphasizing simple fare like tropical fruit juice, homemade bread, and jams made

from papaya, pineapple, and passion fruit. The wide front lawn is spotted with hammocks and mango trees, and gently slopes toward a rocky point, where there's a tide pool big enough to swim in that's filled with small, colorful fish. It's a five-minute walk to the nearest sandy beach, or you can ride horses along the shore.

Thrill seekers will be pleased that Amor de Mar is close to the famed Montezuma Canopy Tour, a zip line that whizzes between trees and down over waterfalls ($35 for two hours). Four miles away, Cabo Blanco Nature Reserve, Costa Rica's oldest nature reserve, covers the tip of the Nicoya Peninsula and is home to howler monkeys, coatis, armadillos, more than 150 varieties of trees, and an assortment of other wildlife. ❶ *Montezuma, 011-506/642-0262, amordemar.com, from $55.*

Right: A patio at
Amor de Mar. Left:
On the grounds.
Following pages:
Amor de Mar at dusk

# Moana Lodge

A massive three-headed tribal sculpture—you kind of have to see it to understand—marks the entrance to Moana, and it's only the first taste of the hotel's African theme. The original owner, a Belgian with Congolese roots, collected angular wooden masks and shields in the Congo and Ivory Coast, and the new Irish owner has taken the motif a step further, adding Zulu shields. They are scattered throughout the property—mounted next to the reception desk and near the pool, where they cast mysterious shadows when the pool is lit in the evening.

> It's the kind of place that would be a blast to take over with friends—particularly ones who can cook

More masks decorate the walls of the seven rooms, and the effect is tribal yet elegant. All rooms have comfortable four-poster, queen-size beds, woven floor mats, and slender tropical flowers in African vases. All of the rooms are air-conditioned, and some have beds with leopard-print pillows.

Located at the southern end of Mal País, on a hill with views of the distant Pacific Ocean, Moana Lodge is blessedly quiet. A shell beach sheltered by old-growth forest is on the other side of the road. Sit in the hot tub, on the sundecks, or by the swimming pool in the shade of a gigantic almond tree, and watch while eagles soar overhead and howler monkeys forage through trees. To get your adrenaline going, rent an ATV from the lodge ($60 per day).

Near enough to Santa Teresa to attract surfers, the lodge is the kind of establishment that would be a blast to take over with a group of close friends—particularly if your friends know how to cook. There's no restaurant on the property, but there is a well-appointed communal kitchen and a self-service bar.
ⓘ *Mal País, 011-506/640-0230, moanalodge.com, from $60. (Kids under the age of 6 are not allowed; kids 6-10 stay at the hotel for free.)*

Left: Moana Lodge's swinging poolside scene. Right: The hotel at night

# The Place

The Swiss owners of The Place have combined the famed tidiness of their home country with design-conscious decor. Of the eight rooms, five are bungalows. Some have mosquito netting hanging from a square frame on the ceiling, which lends a bit of drama, and the private bathrooms have saloon-style doors. Each room is themed without overdoing it: The walls in Ocean Breeze are painted a soothing sky blue, with matching bedding and chair cushions; Beach House is an orange-and-yellow version of Ocean Breeze, evoking the sun and the sand; and Spicy Colors of Mexico has pink walls featuring Mexican art and deep purple, yellow, and orange throw pillows.

*On Tuesdays, there's no need to look for entertainment in town. The Place screens movies over the pool*

The Place bills itself as a surfer hangout, but the crowd is generally more novice than veteran, and many guests sign up for lessons—$45 for two hours, including board rental. (The hotel is on the non-beach side of the street, however, and a 10-minute walk from a good surf break.) The hotel partners with a company called Pura Vida Adventures, hosting week-long surf camps for all levels of female surfers throughout the year.

For non-surfers, a large pool is the focal point of an outdoor living room with lounge chairs, daybeds, and a full bar. The hotel can organize horseback tours along the waterfront or around Mal País, yoga sessions, massages, and a daylong snorkeling trip to Tortuga Island.

A breakfast that includes coffee, fresh fruit, yogurt, granola, and eggs is available for $6 (à la carte options cost more). Other meals can be had in town, a short walk away. On Tuesdays, there's no need to go looking for entertainment in Mal País. The Place hangs a screen over the pool for movie night. ❶ *Mal País, 011-506/640-0001, theplacemalpais.com, from $90.*

**Right: The Place's funky little bar. Left: A piña colada. Following pages: Outdoor movies, and a guest room, at The Place**

# Hotel Milarepa

With its miles of golden beaches, stretches of tropical rain forest, and rocky tide pools, the southern tip of the Nicoya Peninsula is sometimes called the Hawaii of Latin America. Certainly, this small luxury hotel has the aloha spirit. It was either that or the sense of privacy—the hotel has only four rooms—that attracted Leonardo DiCaprio, who once stayed here with a girlfriend.

Caroline Marot and her business partner, Philippe Verquin, filled each of the bungalows with Indonesian teak and bamboo furniture, such as intricately carved armoires and antique four-poster beds, topped by elegant, understated white chair cushions, bedding, and drapery. At night, guests are encouraged to open all of the windows—and the wall of doors that lead to a private veranda—to let in the warm breezes. In the morning, howler monkeys climbing in the trees may provide a comic wake-up call. The tiled bathrooms are private and semi-alfresco: The sink and toilet are under the eaves, but the shower is open to the sky.

This secluded haven is surrounded by activities galore: horseback tours along empty beaches and river valleys, excellent surfing (lessons can be arranged), Saturday night dances, soccer games on Sunday, a canopy tour at the entrance of Cabo Blanco National Park, and sportfishing for yellowfin tuna, red snapper, and mahimahi on a traditional *panga*, or fishing boat. A seven-table restaurant looks out over the pool, past a well-trimmed lawn, and down to the beach, where there's a driftwood massage hut ($60 for over an hour). The American chef, James Kelly, draws from Asian influences and makes great use of local seafood. ⓘ *Santa Teresa, 011-506/640-0023, milarepahotel.com, from $145.*

Left: The pool—and beyond, the beach—at Hotel Milarepa. Right: The hotel's dining area and a guest room bed

# Luz de Vida

Opened in 2003 by a group of seven Israeli friends who wanted to escape city life, Luz de Vida has built up a loyal clientele of surfers, families, and surfing families. Its beachfront access to one of the best surfing breaks in the world might have something to do with that. Another reason for the owners' popularity among the hang-ten set is their dedication to the lifestyle. They'll gladly guide you to the best local beaches and explain each break in detail—handy, considering there are over a hundred within walking distance.

Footpaths lined with coconut, palm, and guava trees lead to the property's 13 air-conditioned cabins. Designed to be a blend of North American cottages and typical jungle bungalows, the cabins use chunky wood furniture and indirect light from wall sconces to create a cozy atmosphere. Three have sleeping lofts, and each has a private patio with two rocking chairs and a hammock.

The view from the pool—past the restaurant, right down to the ocean—is spectacular and can also be enjoyed from the poolside bar. The French-schooled chef uniquely fuses American, Mediterranean, and French cooking styles with occasional seaside accents.

The surf in Santa Teresa is considered some of the Pacific's most consistent, but for the very rare off day, there's a new skate bowl at a nearby surf shop to keep you occupied. Visitors less inclined to risk a broken bone might partake in the hotel's yoga classes, held in an outdoor studio. And Luz de Vida also has a full-service spa, offering massages, peels, manicures, and pedicures. ❶ *Santa Teresa, 011-506/ 640-0320, luzdevida-resort.com, from $95, includes breakfast.*

Right: A cabin veranda
at Luz de Vida. Left:
The secluded pool

# Casa Zen

Experienced surfers, backpacking young couples, and hip parents unafraid to travel with their babies—these are the kinds of free spirits who tend to find common ground at Casa Zen. Kelly Lange, a transplant from Kansas City, Mo., opened the hotel in December 2004. She rents 10 rooms with one or two beds, two dorm rooms, and one room with its own bathroom and kitchen. The other six shared bathrooms could be considered part of Casa Zen's communal ethos. All rooms are spare but inviting, with batik bedspreads and tangerine, ocher, and yellow color schemes.

*Guests hang out in the "rancho," a circular outdoor pavilion with primary-color pillows and comfy banquettes*

Guests usually hang out in the hotel's open-air restaurant, which serves light fare for breakfast and lunch and Thai cuisine for dinner; in the "rancho," a circular outdoor pavilion decked out with primary-color pillows and comfortable banquettes; or in one of the colorful hammocks

that line the walkways. If you'd rather cook your own meals, there's a well-appointed communal kitchen. Games, toys, and a book exchange are available to guests, and the hotel hosts movie nights on Thursdays and Sundays. On weekdays, there are morning yoga sessions ($6 per hour). All this at bargain prices and only 300 feet from the beach.

For those who are interested in getting even closer to nature, Casa Zen also has a small camping area (where spots go for $5 per night). The campers get access to the shared bathrooms, the communal kitchen, and, of course, the hotel's restaurant. ❶ *Santa Teresa, 011-506/640-0523, zencostarica.com, dorm from $12 per person, private rooms from $22, cash only.*

Left: A Casa Zen afternoon. Right: The hotel's open-air pavilion. Following pages: Lunch, and a post-surfing outdoor shower, at Casa Zen

# Point Break Hotel

Point Break Hotel is just off one of the best surf breaks on the Nicoya Peninsula. Experienced surfers, however, will want to know that despite the property's name, it's actually a beach break, not a point break—but non-surfers probably won't care. The owner and his son are both expert surfers who will readily give tips to anyone who asks.

There are seven small teak cabins connected by winding, raised stone paths. The roofs are topped with dried palm fronds and the walls are largely screens; the overall effect is like sleeping out on a porch. The rustic furniture is minimal: Open shelves, tables, and chairs are made from the same type of log beams that form the walls of the cabin. The floors are concrete inlaid with logs. Cotton curtains add a degree of privacy.

Each cabin has a fridge and is fronted by a sandy area with deck chairs for lounging. One slightly larger cabin has its own bathroom and kitchen. The rest share a large bathroom, whose multiple sinks are out in the open. Freestanding showers around the property are handy for rinsing the sand and salt water from you and your gear. The ocean is only 60 feet away, close enough to hear.

For groups of four, there are two cabins lifted high on stilts, each with its own bathroom and kitchen. They look like big, fun tree houses. ❶ *Santa Teresa, 011-506/640-0190, surfing-malpais.com, from $40.*

**Right: Inside a Point Break cabin. Above: Another cabin, with parking right outside**

# Casa Caletas

High atop a bluff, Casa Caletas overlooks the bay where the Coyote River meets the Pacific, and the sunsets can be magical. There's no tourist-friendly town nearby, so guests (many of whom are honeymooners) tend to stay put. The hotel restaurant has a terrific spa-like menu, which features fresh fruits, seafood carpaccios, and green salads. It's read out loud tableside, sometimes by chef Jessica Mora herself.

Everything has been art-directed at Casa Caletas—even the coconuts along the walkways have been painted the resort's signature light green—but it doesn't come off as fussy. An infinity pool takes advantage of the incredible view of the estuary leading to the ocean.

> Everything has been art-directed—even the coconuts along the walkways are painted the signature green

The main house is grand, with high-beamed ceilings, lots of picture windows, and dark rattan furniture. The nine rooms have private patios and striking abstract art made out of reeds. A junior suite, though no bigger than the other rooms, boasts a private hot tub on its porch, as well as views of both the river and the ocean.

There are numerous possible activities—kayaking (boats are available at the hotel's private dock for $10 per hour), horseback riding ($20 per hour), and Jet Skiing ($100 per hour)—but the nearest swimming beach is a mile away. To reach it, you can rent a golf cart for $25 a day. Half-day fishing trips for marlin, mahimahi, and tuna are available; the boat leaves from the hotel.

*San Francisco de Coyote, 011-506/289-6060, casacaletas.com, from $130.*

Left: Casa Caletas's main house. Above: The hotel pool, overlooking the Coyote River

# Tuscany

In a world that gets increasingly frenzied, the slow, bucolic charms of Tuscany—the most famous region in Italy—are impossible to resist. It's one of those rare places that leave every visitor entranced. The scenery casts a spell, of course, what with the stately cypress trees, those rolling hills, the afternoon light turning the fields a rich gold—but there's more to it. Tuscany is the most sophisticated farmland on the planet: The simple pleasures of country life are balanced by truly outstanding food and people who seem to have their priorities right. *La vita* just doesn't get more *dolce* than that.

# La Rignana

A long way from the main roads in Chianti wine country, tucked within 300 acres of forest, olive groves, and vineyards, sits a refined bed-and-breakfast—and working farm—owned by Cosimo Gericke and Sveva Rocco di Torrepadula.

The two historic guesthouses on the property have noble roots. The Fattoria is based on a 1,000-year-old structure that was once a castle. Enlarged in the 18th century, it contains seven rooms with rustic furnishings and sloping brick ceilings laced with wooden beams. The rooms lack televisions, telephones, and air-conditioning, though there is a common area with a stone fireplace that has satellite television and a modem hookup. The other guest building, the two-floor Villa Rignana, belonged to the Ricci family back in the 17th century. During a recent renovation, the owners took great care to preserve the family's aristocratic ornaments. Eight rooms with plank floors and frescoes are available on a nightly basis. (It's possible to rent an entire floor by the week as a single unit—four rooms, each with its own bathroom, with a common kitchen and fireplace.) Both guesthouses are open April through November. The Villa also opens for Christmas.

There's a spare, pretty infinity pool amid the olive trees, with views of rolling hills in the distance. After a freshly brewed Italian espresso, relax outside on a cushioned chair or rent bicycles in town to explore the surrounding area. The winery on the property, where workers employ traditional cultivation techniques (including harvesting the grapes by hand), can be visited by appointment. The hotel's restaurant, in another cluster of farm buildings and under separate management, has tables on a patio and serves traditional Tuscan fare, including wide *papardelle* pasta with wild boar sauce, and delectable *involtini*—thin veal slices wrapped around cheese and prosciutto—stewed with zucchini disks. ❶ *Near Greve in Chianti, 011-39/055-852-065, rignana.it, $133–$177, with a $13 nightly discount for stays of three or more nights, includes breakfast.*

> After an Italian espresso, relax outside on a cushioned chair or rent bicycles in town and explore the surrounding area

Left: La Rignana's pool. Right: A farmhouse table. Previous pages: Looking out onto a patio at La Rignana. Following pages: A sitting room at La Rignana

# Podere Terreno

Roberto Melosi left a promising hotel career at London's Savoy to become chef and host of an *agriturismo*—an inn on a working farm in Italy. His Paris-born wife, Marie-Sylvie Haniez, who had owned a modern-art gallery in Florence, decided the only proper way to run an *agriturismo* was to share communal dinners with guests in the French table d'hôte style. Together, the couple manages a restored

> Wine means a lot to the family: Vineyards encircle the house, and rooms are named after local grapes

16th-century farmhouse that has seven country-comfy rooms furnished with a hodgepodge of carved-wood vanities and worn terra-cotta floors. Credit for the vineyard's light, organic Chianti classico goes to Marie-Sylvie's adult son, Pier Francesco, who gave up dirt-bike racing to study viticulture and enology at the University of Florence.

Wine means a lot to the family: Vineyards encircle the house, and guest rooms are named for local grapes. Malvasia, Trebbiano, Vernaccia, and Ciliegiolo are all on the east side of the house, which has the best vineyard views. In summer, guests enjoy that same view from the patio during three-hour family-style dinners that may include lasagna, steaks, and stuffed tomatoes. Roberto and Marie-Sylvie sit at either end of the long wooden table and do their best to keep the conversation lively, in multiple languages if necessary.

A short stroll will take you to a small lake located on the estate, a favorite spot for bird and fish watching. On cooler days, dinner moves inside to a common room,

where copper pots dangle from thick wood beams and the stone walls are decorated with oil paintings and ceramics, not to mention Marie-Sylvie's collection of sun icons. The room's seven-foot fireplace, which dates back to the 14th century, is surrounded by armchairs and a sofa where Lola (Roberto and Marie-Sylvie's setter mix) is happy to while away the hours at your feet. In 2004, Podere Terreno's somewhat simple operation got a little bit swankier, inaugurating a wine-tasting cantina and a tiny spa with a hot tub and massage table. ⓘ *Near Radda in Chianti, 011-39/0577-738-312, podereterreno. it, $240, includes breakfast and dinner.*

Right: The Malvasia room.
Left: Podere Terreno's wine.
Following pages: Dinner, and a nap, at Podere Terreno

# Castello di Gargonza

On the crest of a hill enveloped by forest sits a fairy-tale castle with a 13th-century hamlet curled around the base of a crenellated tower. The hilltop village is Gargonza, fought over for centuries by Florentines and Sienese, host to an exiled Dante in the early 1300s—and now entirely for rent. Gargonza's 22 houses, which like the castle are built of pale stone, serve as apartments, and most feature original working fireplaces, kitchenettes, and 17th-century-style furnishings. There are also 10 simple doubles (no kitchens or fireplaces).

Converting the place into lodgings for tourists was the only way Count Roberto Guicciardini—whose ancestors have been lords of the castle since 1700—could save the decaying village after the last of its farmers and artisans abandoned Gargonza in the 1960s. Lovingly restored by local residents using only indigenous materials, each apartment is named in honor of one of its former occupants. You have to leave your car outside the village walls—this is now entirely a pedestrian town. The central courtyard, with an old well and geraniums spilling from arcaded balconies, is a sort of open-air living room. The old olive-press building is sometimes a performance space for impromptu concerts by guests or visiting musicians. It also functions as a common room with sofas, a television, and the breakfast buffet.

Just outside the town's medieval walls is a swimming pool surrounded by fragrant rosemary bushes and olive and cypress trees, as well as the excellent restaurant, located on the former site of the village's grain thresher—also the staging ground for an occasional game of bocce. Owner Neri Guicciardini, one of the count's sons, adds innovative flair to Tuscan classics on the restaurant's menu. Guests can enjoy their meal by the fireplace in the large dining room or outside on the even grander covered terrace. A Romanesque parish church built in the 13th century contains a fresco from 1415 and still holds mass every Sunday. ❶ *West of Monte San Savino, less than a mile off the road between Arezzo and Siena, 011-39/0575-847-021, gargonza.it, $139–$229 in B&B, daily apartment rental (without use of kitchen) $186–$349, weekly apartment rentals (with kitchen) $848–$2,165, includes breakfast.*

**Left: The Castello di Gargonza's medieval tower. Right: A stylish interior. Following pages: The Castello's pool and its owner, Count Roberto Guicciardini**

# Fattoria di Vagli

After two miles of dirt road winding through dense woods, a cypress-lined driveway leads to a 17th-century farmhouse surrounded by grapevines and fields that rotate between corn, wheat, spelt, and sunflowers. The Vagli farm is a family operation where the mission is to preserve traditional varieties of local plants and farm animals. Carla Ferri oversees the daily operations; her father tends the crops; her uncles shepherd the free-range pigs, cows, rabbits, ducks, chickens, and pigeons; her brother cures the meats; and her mother works in the kitchen cooking for guests and the family ($23 for three courses plus dessert, without wine). Almost all of the ingredients used in meals are straight from the farm, right down to the olive oil and aromatic herbs used to season the dishes—even the firewood is from the property.

Carla looks after guests and the 10 rooms, furnished in a simple country style with hand-painted headboards and rough wooden beams. The rooms on the ground floor have exposed stone walls and are a bit smaller, but the abundance of light from large windows makes them feel airy. The suite with a fireplace costs $21 more, while the two units that share a bathroom cost $10

less—though those two also interconnect, so they're perfect for families.

There are five bicycles that guests may use for free, and the dining room walls are lined with topographical maps to help them plan hikes and rides throughout the region—or just within the woodlands that cover most of Vagli's 800 acres. The grounds are so extensive that some visitors never realize there's a swimming pool hidden next to the fruit orchard. Once a week, a member of the family takes guests on a tour of the farming operation, which produces figs, olives, prosciutto, and more. Carla will also make arrangements for guided hikes within the Castelvecchio nature reserve, which overlaps with the farm and includes the ruins of a medieval castle and village. ❶ *In Libbiano, north of San Gimignano, 011-39/0577-946-025, naturaesalute.it, $92, includes breakfast.*

Right: A room at Fattoria di Vagli. Left: On the estate's 800 acres. Following pages: The owner's mother making a batch of peach marmalade

# Giovanni da Verrazzano

Saturday is market day in the village of Greve in Chianti, when the main piazza is buzzing with vendors selling fruit, vegetables, *porchetta* (pork) sandwiches, and everyday necessities. The stalls are arranged around the statue of local sailor Giovanni da Verrazzano, the first European to discover New York Harbor. For the past 800 years, the hotel now named in this hometown hero's honor has watched over daily life on the triangular piazza.

The location and the views are what set the hotel apart. The 10 guest rooms are basic, though terra-cotta floors and painted metal bedsteads are standard. For some rooms the private bathroom is down the hall. The front rooms overlook the bustling square, while those in the back (Nos. 4–7) have little private terraces with vistas over lichen-spotted roof tiles to the vast hills beyond. A larger room upstairs (No. 10), with its sloping ceilings and Persian rugs, claims similar views over the hills, although it doesn't have a balcony.

Greve is noteworthy as one of the first "Citta Slow" or Slow Cities, which are dedicated to protecting original architecture, local culture, and small-town life by promoting small businesses and local industries. The Slow Cities have been inspired by the Slow Food movement, and traditional cooking is an integral part of Greve's lifestyle. The hotel's restaurant, on a terrace atop one of the piazza's arcades, has fed hungry visitors to Greve since 1200. For guests who want to absorb the true flavor of the region, the hotel offers cooking classes in English; students learn to select quality ingredients, prepare a Tuscan meal, and choose a wine that will complement it. ❶ *Greve, 011-39/055-853-189, verrazzano. it, $133, includes breakfast.*

> The hotel's restaurant, on a terrace atop one of the piazza's arcades, has fed hungry visitors to Greve since 1200

**Left: The restaurant at Giovanni da Verrazzano overlooks the town's piazza. Right: A table with a view**

# Il Poderuccio

Il Poderuccio lies down the road from Sant'Angelo in Colle, a hilltop medieval village in the heart of Brunello wine country. Don't be alarmed if there's no one around when you stroll across the lawn to the check-in desk. Owner Giorgio Girardi could be in the back tinkering with the tractor or in the fields pruning the grapevines, while his wife, Renate, is probably in one of the gardens.

The Girardis rely entirely on word-of-mouth to guide discriminating travelers to their doorstep. Giorgio left an international banking career to restore this farm and is proud to have strung grapevines along only a fifth of his land.

Locals think that he's insane to limit his production of one of the country's most famous (and most expensive) wines, but Giorgio prefers keeping the operation small enough to run almost single-handedly.

Renate has filled the six large guest rooms with many thoughtful touches, including mosquito screens (which are rare in Italy), plenty of towels, and, sometimes, garlands of dried lavender perched on the windowsills. Throughout the rosemary-filled property, there are pretty nooks, benches waiting under shade trees, a well-sheltered swimming pool in the olive grove, and stacks of perfectly arranged wood.

In cool weather, breakfast is served on the hotel's sunny front porch; during the summer, however, the action shifts to the back patio, with views straight out of a Renaissance painting—distant mountains above green and gold fields striped with vines and spiked here and there with Tuscany's iconic cypress trees.

ℹ️ *Colle, six miles south of Montalcino, 011-39/0577-844-052, $114, includes breakfast, open Easter–November (closed for July in some years).*

Left: Breakfast alfresco at Il Poderuccio. Right: In the vineyard. Following pages: A picnic spot and a rustic hearth

# Caribbean

The vast majority of visitors to the Caribbean stay on cruise ships or at big resorts. While both have an appeal—namely, ease and amenities—there's something to be said for thinking small. What you gain might be worth more than what you lose. Don't expect conga lines and limbo contests; at the hotels in this chapter, you have no choice but to relax. And since the hotels are often in remote areas, you're able to have a more authentic Caribbean (or Bahamian) experience. Best of all, it's guaranteed that you'll end up meeting locals— and not just ones wearing starched uniforms. If there's one thing that's un-Caribbean, it's starch.

# Rockhouse Hotel

Seclusion isn't easy to come by in the party town of Negril, Jamaica, with its sprawling resorts and thumping dance beats, but that's exactly what Rockhouse delivers, primarily to hip couples and families hoping to avoid anything remotely resembling the stereotypical spring break experience.

Rockhouse's rounded thatched villas are strung atop a low cliff carved with stairs that lead to the warm waters of Pristine Cove. The 18 private units peeking out of the jungle right at the cliff's edge start at $295 in winter, but the long buildings set a bit farther back are easier to pull off—six studios with sea views ($150) and nine standard rooms with garden views ($125), all with minibars, safes, air-conditioning, mosquito netting around four-poster beds, and furniture constructed from local timber.

*The paths inevitably lead to quiet nooks, isolated beach chairs, and what people say are the best sunset views in Jamaica*

Guests take yoga classes, chill out at the 60-foot infinity pool (where lunch is served from an open barbecue), and stroll the property's serpentine paths, which inevitably lead to quiet nooks, isolated beach

chairs, and what many people say are the best sunset views in Jamaica. At Pristine Cove, guests can swim and snorkel around dwarf tube sponges, small coral heads, and reef fish; the pool bar rents snorkeling gear. The action on Seven Mile Beach—including live reggae on the beach at Alfred's (Tuesday, Friday, and Sunday) and Roots Bamboo (where the schedule varies)—is a quick cab ride away.

Closer to home, and suspended dramatically over the waterfront, is the Rockhouse Restaurant. It serves New Jamaican cuisine that incorporates native, Chinese, Spanish, English, and Indian flavors. Another option, right next door, is Pirate's Cave, where patrons eat grilled lobster before jumping off the cliff and swimming into the sea cave underneath. ℹ *Negril, Jamaica, 876/957-4373, rockhousehotel.com, from $125.*

**Right: A catnap at the Rockhouse. Left: The hotel's coastline. Previous pages: Stone stairs lead from the Rockhouse to the water**

# Jake's

Sitting alongside rocky shoals washed by the warm surf of Jamaica's South Coast, Jake's Easter egg–colored guest cottages are funky boutique versions of the Caribbean shack. The two dozen buildings overflow with odd, endearing details that are an exercise in culture-clash chic: Indian minaret–shaped windows, Arabian-influenced domes, hammered-tin doors, door frames made with driftwood, Mayan-inspired weavings, glass bottles embedded in plaster walls. The grounds are dotted with flowering bushes and desert greenery—cacti, yuccas, gnarled little trees.

What you get instead of a room with a television, air-conditioning, and a phone is a welcoming, laid-back vibe. (And don't bother trying to find Jake, a parrot who's not around anymore—it's a long story.) The hotel was created by Sally Henzell, a theater designer by trade, and is currently run by her son Jason; both are particularly loved by the surrounding fishing village for starting a non-profit organization that pays for medical rescue services, school computers, fishing tournaments, and even literary festivals where Shakespeare is performed in Jamaican patois. Consequently, the bar and pool at Jake's are popular with guests and locals alike, and hustlers are virtually nonexistent.

Boats have been raised on stilts and capped with thatched roofs to create the hotel's open-air restaurant, Little Ochie, located right on the beach. You can choose your own fresh fish, lobster, crab, or octopus, and the proprietor, Blackie, will cook it any way you like. To really soak up the south shore culture, sign up for a cooking lesson with one of the hotel's chefs and learn the secrets of Jamaican specialties such as jerk meats, ackee, and "run down," a traditional island dish made with mackerel and coconut milk ($20 per person). *South Coast, Jamaica, 800/688-7678, islandoutpost.com/jakes, from $115.*

**Left: The barefoot bar at Jake's. Right: A minaret-shaped window at the hotel**

# Country Country

The 20 cottages at Country Country form a tiny village on a narrow acre covered with tropical gardens in the middle of Negril's hopping Seven Mile Beach.

No two cottages are the same, though air-conditioning, ceiling fans, louvered shutters, a porch, and a cabinet hiding a tea set, television, and refrigerator are standard. Other than that, you might find bamboo bed frames, whimsical murals of starfish, or a fleet of conch shells surrounding the windows. The walls and gingerbread trim are painted in bright shades of yellow. Sisal rugs lie beneath either a king-size bed or two twins, and the loud bedspreads somehow go better than one would expect with the purple lamp shades spangled with yellow stars.

*Most of the cottages are stand-alone buildings with neat little gardens and cool stone floors*

Most cottages are stand-alone buildings with neat little gardens and cool stone floors, but a few are double-deckers. Second-floor units come with hardwood floors and views over the vegetation to the water (it's $20 more a night to stay upstairs or in the single-story cottages closest to the water).

Country Country's Jamaican owners recently acquired adjacent land and plan on doubling the number of cottages and installing a pool and tennis courts.

At the edge of the beach, there's an open-air, thatched-roof bar and restaurant that serves ackee, cod fish, jerk chicken, and fruity drinks. Jimmy Buffett's Margaritaville, a two-minute walk from the hotel, has a more festive atmosphere.

Guests can negotiate trips and transportation to popular sites with drivers who are on the property daily; the front desk will also arrange tours upon request. One fairly popular option, an hour's drive from the hotel, is to take a safari boat up the Black River, a lazy waterway that's home to many birds and animals, including crocodiles. ❶ *Negril, Jamaica, 888/790-5264, countryjamaica.com, from $160.*

**Right: A private terrace at Country Country. Left: One of the hotel's many whimsical details**

# Seascape Inn

Most of Andros Island is uninhabitable Bahamian marshland, choked by mangroves and shot through with so many lakes and channels that from the air it looks like a doily. The Seascape Inn, on Andros Island's Mangrove Cay, is within minutes of a 120-mile-long barrier reef (the third largest in the world), making it perfect for diving, fishing, or just dropping out for a week.

The five raised cabanas are paragons of simplicity: They have white walls, white bedspreads, and white curtains; open-beamed ceilings; and terra-cotta floor tiles. Furniture consists of a bed and a wooden armchair; the only real amenity, if you can call it that, is a ceiling fan. In other words, there's hardly anything to distract from the miles of deserted white-sand beach.

When not lolling on their decks, guests pass the hours bonefishing from the flats in front of their bungalows, exploring the reef by kayak, or pedaling along Mangrove Cay's lone road (bikes and kayaks are free for guests).

Brooklyn-born hosts Mickey and Joan McGowan can typically be found at the bar and restaurant, which serves basic fare: burgers and quesadillas for lunch, and steaks, chicken Parmesan, and fresh fish for dinner. Gracious and friendly, the McGowans are clearly thrilled with their choice to move to the Bahamas 10 years ago. Mickey, who sports an impressive collection of cheeky T-shirts, is a PADI-certified scuba instructor and takes guests out most mornings on his 34-foot boat for a two-tank dive ($100). Joan likes to garden and bake, whipping up muffins and biscuits at dawn and tempting desserts—sometimes pies made with coconuts from the yard—in the afternoon. The rest of the family is four-legged: Bernie, Bebe, Dot, and Magoo, a quartet of abandoned dogs rescued and spoiled silly by the McGowans. ❶ *Andros Island, Bahamas, 242/369-0342, seascapeinn.com, from $140 (includes continental breakfast).*

Left: An Andros sunset.
Right: One of five cabanas
at Seascape Inn, on Andros
Island in the Bahamas

# Staniel Cay Yacht Club

In the center of the Bahamas' 100-mile-long Exuma island chain, a half-hour flight from Nassau, is tiny Staniel Cay. A popular port for the sailing set, the island is home to only 80 full-time residents. The Staniel Cay Yacht Club, a five-minute golf-cart ride from the airstrip (there are only a handful of cars on the island), has been providing casual, comfortable accommodations since 1956. Couples and families love the nine pastel-colored cottages, seven of which have private balconies that jut over the stunning crystal-clear water.

There's a brand-new swimming pool and sundeck, a small beach next door, and more dramatic stretches of sand accessible by foot or golf cart, but most people are here to play skipper. The club has an 18-slip marina, and a Boston Whaler is docked outside each cottage; guests are given a map and encouraged to explore on their own. There are a ton of deserted islands nearby and one very important unspoken rule: If a beach is occupied, you should move on to the next one. Thunderball Grotto, where part of the James Bond film *Thunderball* was shot, is a favorite for snorkeling. Just north of the grotto, at Major Spot, surf-swimming pigs (yes, pigs) will circle your boat, expecting to be fed. Four miles or so beyond Major there's a group of tame nurse sharks who don't mind posing for pictures.

After your day's excursions, return to the clubhouse for a drink at the casual island bar, named one of Jimmy Buffett's "10 Great Places for a Waterside Drink," in *USA Today*. In the restaurant, dinner is served in traditional Bahamian style: Diners place their orders ahead of time and are seated en masse at the ringing of a dinner bell. Though you can pay for lodging and extras à la carte, a package that covers lodging, all meals, taxes and gratuities, a Whaler (with fuel), a golf cart, snorkeling gear, and round-trip transfers is often the better value. The Yacht Club also offers charter flights from Fort Lauderdale ($462 round trip), and you can be here from the mainland in two hours—instead of just wishing that you were. ❶ *Staniel Cay, Bahamas, 954/467-8920, stanielcay.com, from $210.*

Left: Aerial view of the Exumas. Right: A cottage with a view at Staniel Cay in the Bahamas

# Villa Beach Cottages

The hour-and-a-half ride from St. Lucia's international airport to the Villa Beach Cottages in a standard taxi is $75, but you'll save $10 if you let one of the Villa Beach drivers do the honors. He or she will also chat you up and buy you a cold Piton—St. Lucia's local brew—along the way. The special treatment is one of the reasons owner Colin Hunte's 20 villas welcome so many repeat guests, some having visited regularly for 20 years.

The operation dates to 1958, when Hunte's grandfather bought two former U.S. Air Force barracks and had them moved to a 40-foot-wide beach on the island's northwestern tip. Colin took over 16 years ago, but he's tried to keep the feel of the original complex. A manicured lawn and concrete stone paths end at a low retaining wall at the edge of the beach. New buildings have incorporated cathedral ceilings, jalousie shutters, and gingerbread woodwork. Villas have handcrafted wooden furniture and four-poster beds. Literature lovers can stay in the Nobel Villa, featuring the watercolors of 1992 Nobel laureate Derek Wolcott, who spent his holidays in residence.

Most of the rentals have a private patio with ocean views (on a clear day you can see the island of Martinique). There are two pools, or for true relaxation, snag one of the hammocks slung between the coconut trees at the water's edge and drift off to the sounds of the waves. When you get hungry, head next door to the Wharf, which makes an exemplary roti, the spicy Jamaican wrap filled with vegetables, chicken, or beef. ℹ️ *St. Lucia, 758/450-2884, villabeachcottages.com, from $210.*

**Left:** The Pitons and town of Soufriere. **Right:** The quiet, homey decor of Villa Beach Cottages

# Casa La Lanchita

This three-story guesthouse is just north of the main town, Isabel Segunda, on the Puerto Rican island of Vieques. Its location, on a cliff overlooking a white-sand beach and a coral reef, gives its eight air-conditioned suites panoramic views of the Atlantic, which is just 30 feet away.

The rooms feature rattan furniture, decorative screens, and louvered windows, and most have a glass-brick wall that creates a private sleeping area while letting in natural light. Each has a living room/kitchen, which for even the most reluctant chef is a draw. (Food is still Vieques' low point.) Casa La Lanchita's kitchens are fully equipped, and the closest market is easy to reach on foot.

Marikay and Doug McHoul, who live in an attached apartment, have owned the place for 20 years and are famous for happily going above and beyond the call of duty. Doug tends to be generous with the late-night beers and has been known to lend a hand with flat tires.

There's a pool built into the top of the seawall. Just down the coast, swimming, snorkeling, and surfing are possible at Lanchita Beach. The guesthouse has coolers and beach chairs available for guests.

La Lanchita is within walking distance of shops, bars, and an Internet café—a relief on an island where almost everything requires a drive. One attraction worth the time in a car (and one every visitor will want to see) is Bioluminescent Bay, where the seawater is magically aglow with millions of phosphorescent microorganisms.

ⓘ *Vieques, Puerto Rico, 800/774-4717, viequeslalanchita.com, from $95.*

**Right: All smiles at Casa La Lanchita. Left: A guest room, and owners Marikay and Doug McHoul. Following pages: Casa La Lanchita**

# Hacienda Tamarindo

After one too many Vermont winters, Burr Vail and his wife, Linda, moved to Vieques in 1995 and converted a restaurant and dance hall into Hacienda Tamarindo. It's named for the 250-year-old tree that the lobby's atrium was built around, and below which breakfast is served.

Some of the rooms are designed around a theme: The watermelon room sports watermelon-patterned quilts and watermelon-shaped decorative baskets and accents. Linda, a former interior designer, is responsible for the antique wooden signs and vintage movie posters.

*Burr knows the island of Vieques inside and out. His hour-long morning lectures are essential for intelligent vacationing*

Along with the resident talking parrot, Shaboo, and Barkley the sheepdog, Burr usually joins guests at the big breakfast: eggs, bacon, hash browns, fruit, toast, juice, and coffee. Burr knows the island of Vieques inside and out. His hour-long morning lectures are essential for intelligent vacationing. Among his many pearls of wisdom: Green Beach usually has too many sand flies to make it worth visiting in the afternoon; to find Secret Beach, look for the spray-painted metal trash can.

Guests soak in the full-size freshwater pool with panoramic views amid coconut and mahogany trees, or head to Sun Bay Beach for a swim, only five minutes by car. A stone path leads from the hacienda down to the waterfront, which, while not safe for swimming, is ideal for beach-combing or a leisurely stroll. Housekeeper Rosa packs beach-bound guests a lunch, more than making up for the lack of kitchenettes.

Hacienda Tamarindo is an eight-minute drive from the 18,000-acre Vieques National Wildlife Refuge, the largest such refuge in the Caribbean. Formerly a naval base, the area is home to the pristine Red, Blue, Garcia, Secret, and Orchid Beaches. Leatherback and hawksbill sea turtles can often be spotted. Sections of the refuge are open from sunrise to sunset. ❶ *787/741-0420, haciendatamarindo.com, from $175, no young children.*

Left: Hacienda Tamarindo at dusk. Right: Chilling on the patio. Following pages: Goats outside Hacienda Tamarindo, and a room at the hotel

# La Finca Caribe

It makes sense that J. Crew would chose Vieques's La Finca as a location for two catalog shoots. In the proprietor's words, La Finca is "one part funky summer camp, one part homey wilderness lodge," and flowing linen fabrics and casual-looking models fit right in on the hippieish yet manicured property. Most of the staff are the temporarily relocated, always barefoot friends of owners Anne Isaak (a restaurateur in New York) and Corky Merwin (a creative director who lives in Seattle).

> The owner calls La Finca "one part funky summer camp, one part homey wilderness lodge"

Three rustic houses are spread across three hilly acres. The hospitality is warm, but a bit devil-may-care; don't expect phones, televisions, or matching towels or bedsheets. Hand-painted folk-art accents decorate the floor in the library/common area, and the wraparound deck is where the action is: There's a self-serve honor bar, a grill, a porch swing, hammocks, and laundry facilities, with a horseshoe pit below. Banana, star fruit, and mango trees frame the small swimming pool.

Visitors pass their days playing volleyball and Scrabble, swimming, grilling fish, and hanging out under the randomly strung fairy lights at the picnic table by the pool. The hotel is the kind of place where you get to know your fellow guests, who come from all around the world. Then again, a certain degree of familiarity is to be expected when you're showering side by side in the outdoor stalls.

La Finca is an especially good value for groups. For $525 to $700 a week, two or three people can share the casita; for $750 to $1,000, a family can rent the cabana, which sleeps up to four (both have private kitchens, bathrooms, and decks). Groups of up to 20, meanwhile, can take over the entire six-room main house for $2,600 to $3,500. ❶ *Vieques, Puerto Rico, 787/741-0495, lafinca.com, from $60.*

Right: La Finca Caribe's Treehouse Bar. Left: A guest room. Following pages: Hanging out and running free at La Finca Caribe

# French Riviera

Few places on earth have as glamorous a reputation as the French Riviera—whether you're looking at a tabloid from the '50s or this year, you'll find candid shots of celebs (Brigitte Bardot! Jay-Z!) living it up on yachts and at beachside nightclubs. But you don't have to be walking the red carpet at Cannes to enjoy the Côte d'Azur. The coastline has a quiet, romantic side, especially if you venture inland—even if it's just a couple of miles. The hard edges start to mellow out, and the traffic fumes give way to wildflowers. The result feels like the best of both worlds—it's a fantasyland that has both sizzle and soul.

# Hôtel Napoléon

On the Bay of Garavan, about a 10-minute walk from the center of Menton, this bit of affordable chic is just across the street from the beach—and less than a mile from the Italian border. (You can jog there on your morning run.)

Rooms are airy and look crisp and modern; most are decorated with red bedspreads and curtains with broad red-and-white vertical stripes. All rooms have air-conditioning, satellite television, minibars, and Internet access. It's worth spending extra for a room facing the sea—you'll be rewarded with a great view and a wooden balcony with a table and chairs. Three suites have panoramic views over the bay. A road lines the entire seafront, but once the double-paned windows are closed, the whoosh of traffic is gone. Breakfast is a buffet served on the downstairs patio; guests sit at café tables under white canvas umbrellas and banana trees, or in the red-and-white breakfast room. There are soft, square, white armchairs in the 24-hour lounge at the hotel bar, and a large plasma-screen television for watching sporting events. A small fitness area is located right next to the pool, handy for cooling off after a workout.

For the true Riviera experience, you should consider renting a lounge chair and umbrella ($19 per day) on the private beach—look for the large pineapple formed with palm fronds. Then have a waiter from the beach restaurant bring you something refreshing to drink. If that's not enough, the hotel even has its own ice-cream parlor next to the beach. In the afternoon and evening, lunch and dinner are served at the water's edge. Tables are adorned with animal-print cloths and decorative mosquito nets are draped artfully about. Every Wednesday from mid-June to mid-September the hotel hosts entertaining themed parties. ❶ *Menton, 011-33/4-93-35-89-50, napoleon-menton.com, $112–$162.*

**Left: Hôtel Napoléon.**
**Right: Sunbathing by the**
**pool. Previous pages:**
**The town of Menton as**
**seen from Hôtel Napoléon**

# Les Deux Frères

Go up—past the crowds, past the noise—to the tiny village of Roquebrune-Cap-Martin. Stop to gasp at the panorama from the tiny town square, and notice the lovely dining terrace to your right. It's attached to the restaurant of the intimate Les Deux Frères, in a 19th-century stone building that was once a school. A mahogany bar fills the lobby; a narrow staircase leads up to the 10 small, pretty rooms.

Each guest room has a name indicating its theme. The African room, for instance, has carved-wood furniture, bed linens with banana trees pictured on them, and a leopard-print headboard and chair cushions. The Marine room has a nautical theme: Blue and white stripes abound, and there are small porthole-shaped lamps above the bed. The Bride room is white-on-white, with a romantic padded headboard, a white wrought-iron café table and chairs, and a wrought-iron lamp draped with crystals.

The hotel's views range from lovely to stupendous. Depending on your room's orientation, you might look out toward the Roquebrune-Cap-Martin town square, the rugged hills, or—if you get the full frontal—the cliffs, the sea, and, in the distance, the principality of Monaco.

The surrounding area has many sandy beaches to choose from, and even more charming villages to visit. There is a 10th-century château not too far away, and it's open for public tours in the summer months. ℹ️ *Roquebrune-Cap-Martin, 011-33/4-93-28-99-00, lesdeuxfreres.com, $94–$138.*

Right: A room at Les Deux Frères. Left: The façade. Following pages: The view from Les Deux Frères, and the hotel's knight watchman

## VENCE
# Auberge des Seigneurs

A former tavern and postal relay, the Auberge des Seigneurs, tucked away on a side street, has six large, high-ceilinged rooms for rent, each named for a painter, with beautiful views of the hills or the rooftops of the village. Decorative objects, antiques, and flowers are plentiful; the hotel manages to retain a feel of old Provence without coming off as kitsch.

The 400-year-old walls are painted white, setting off the rustic ceiling beams, the bold curtains, and the dark wood furniture. Oriental rugs are scattered over the *tomettes*, the octagonal terra-cotta tiles that cover the floors of old buildings all over the south of France. There are flowers and fruit in every guest room, but no Internet connection, no televisions, and no air-conditioning (which the thick walls make unnecessary, anyhow).

> The specialty is roasted chicken, cooked by the owner right over an open flame in the fireplace

Downstairs, copper pots, pans, and bed warmers hang over a wood-manteled fireplace. Through a large wooden door is the wonderful restaurant, where the specialty is roasted chicken, cooked by the owner over an open flame in the fireplace. Out front is a flower-bedecked square, and just behind, through the back entrance, you'll find the old city of Vence. Known as the "City of Art," Vence has winding streets, shops, artists' galleries, and cafés. Most notably, it's also home to a cathedral with a mosaic created by Marc Chagall, who lived in the town for 16 years. ⓘ *Vence, 011-33/ 4-93-58-04-24, $100–$126, closed November–February.*

Right: The restaurant at Auberge des Seigneurs. Above: Auberge des Seigneurs's front door, and one of the six rooms

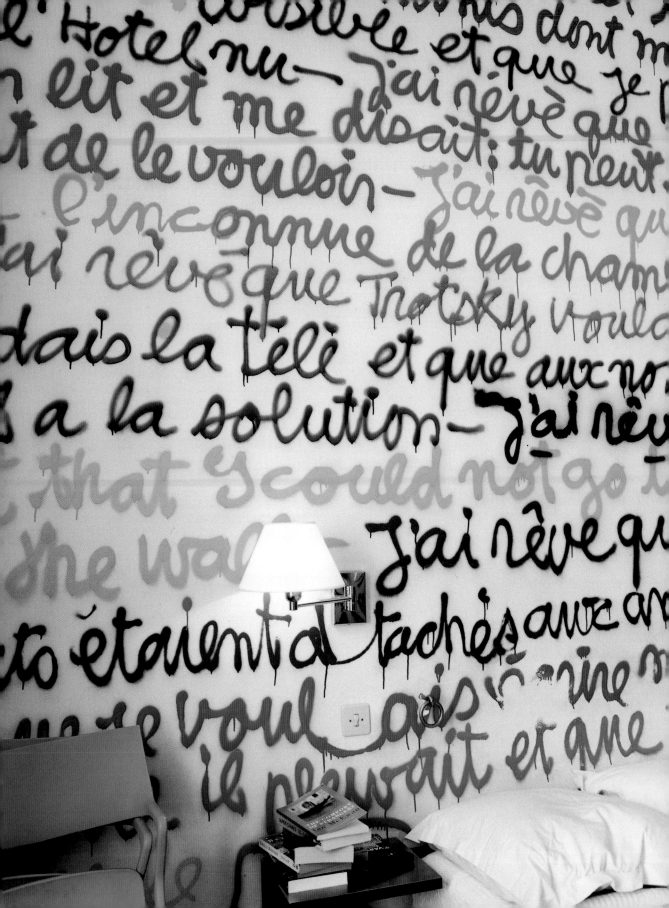

# Hôtel Windsor

Owned by the art-loving Redolfi family since 1942, the Windsor fits somewhere between classic Nice accommodations and an artist's loft. A massive Chinese Imperial bed frame decorates the lobby, while the elevator has a rocket-themed photo collage and a liftoff soundtrack. Several members of the multilingual staff speak excellent English and are happy to answer questions, give directions, and recommend local restaurants and activities.

Artists designed almost half of the 57 rooms. One is adorned with colorful writing, and guests are invited to record their dreams in a book. Another is a bare room papered in gold leaf, with a glowing white double bed. A third is all white save for two gray pillows on the bed and large yellow words—*almost*, *beyond*, and *somehow*, among others—on the wall. (The artist rendered them in yellow to "reflect the sun in Nice" and would like guests staying in the room to interpret the larger meaning of the words.) Yet another room is inspired by two elephants: Babar and Ganesh. There are other artists' rooms that aren't quite as conceptually demanding, the primary element being tropical murals. Book a "superior" room on the garden side of the hotel—the standard rooms facing the road can be noisy, especially whenever a bus passes by.

The hotel has suitably modern accoutrements, including Internet access in the lobby, a small stainless-steel bar with molded plastic stools, and a fitness area on the top floor, where you can have a massage or enjoy a sauna for an extra fee. A garden surrounds the plunge pool, and a rocky beach is a few blocks away. The hotel is in a great location; the Promenade des Anglais and Old Town are nearby, as are many quality restaurants. ❶ *Nice, 011-33/4-93-88-59-35, hotelwindsornice.com, $144–$188.*

**Left: Getting artsy at Hôtel Windsor. Right: The fitness area. Following pages: Another guest room, and the bar at the Windsor**

# La Jabotte

Adorable is the only way to describe this one-story villa with its three bungalows clustered around a garden shaded by orange trees. Though lacking air-conditioning and not at all luxurious, each of the 12 smallish rooms has been decorated in a manner that's usually reserved for high-class accommodations—rich colors on the walls, original artwork (including paintings by one of the owners), and imaginative choices of furniture and fixtures. Some rooms have distinct themes: birds, calligraphy, flowers, angels.

> In spring and summer, the owners host cocktail hour in the courtyard. Tommy, the hotel's Westie, often joins in the fun.

Breakfast receives equal attention. The orange juice is fresh-squeezed, with fruit that comes from the hotel's trees, and the jam and pastries are homemade. An amicable affair where guests tend to socialize, breakfast can be taken in the courtyard or in the lobby, which resembles a cross between a living room and a crafts boutique (the paintings and ceramics are nearly all for sale). Owners Yves April and

Claude Mora aim to recreate what they describe as the "friendly spirit" of a *chambre d'hôte*, a private home that rents out rooms. During the spring and summer, they host cocktail hour in the courtyard, serving champagne and wine-based concoctions with light appetizers. (Tommy, the hotel's Westie, often joins in the fun.)

Though La Jabotte is in a quiet residential neighborhood, the beach is only 60 yards from the hotel. Old Antibes is an easy 10-minute walk, and a marina and nautical club are close by. There's always something going on: The town of Juan-les-Pins hosts the International Jazz Festival every July, an antiques fair is held in March or April, and August brings a fireworks festival. In fact, there's a festival of some kind just about every month—that's life on the Côte d'Azur.

ℹ *Cap d'Antibes, 011-33/4-93-61-45-89, jabotte.com, $82–$131, includes breakfast.*

**Right:** Outside La Jabotte.
**Left:** A good-night wish.
**Following pages:** A window at La Jabotte, and Tommy, the owners' Westie

# Hôtel le Mas des Brugassières

The most stressful thing about staying at Hôtel le Mas des Brugassières is pronouncing the name. Once you've managed that (broo-gah-si-*ehr*), it's simply a matter of throwing your luggage on the hand-quilted *boutis* bedspread, freshening up in the large bathroom, heading out to a cushioned chair or the hammock by the pool, and ordering yourself a drink.

Nine twisty miles inland from the glorious chaos of Saint-Tropez, the low-key hotel is in the Massif des Maures, a sparsely populated region of low mountains, scrubby pine forests, and an occasional vineyard. Biking, hiking, and horseback riding are all available nearby; the beaches of Sainte-Maxime are five miles away. You can also rent catamarans and sailboards there—or take in a movie or show. If golf is your game, you'll find a pair of courses to test your skills.

The two-story hotel, which is closed mid-October through March, is based on a classic Provençal *mas*, or house. Each of the 14 comfortable rooms has air-conditioning, a private entrance, and a patio or terrace with table and chairs. They are beautifully decorated with attractive bed throws and tapestries, candles, and fresh flowers. There's free Wi-Fi in the public areas—the pool, reception, and the lounge. Take breakfast on your terrace or next to the pool under the olive trees. (Breakfast is served until noon and is mandatory in high season, which raises the rate by $10 per person.) After breakfast, play a game of table tennis or *pétanque*—or just work on your tan. ℹ *Plan-de-la-Tour, 011-33/4-94-55-50-55, mas-des-brugassieres.com, $98–$119.*

Right: Breakfast at the Mas des Brugassières. Left: The façade, which evokes a farmhouse. Following pages: The hotel's backyard, and a room

# Hôtel Brise Marine

On the terribly exclusive Saint-Jean-Cap-Ferrat peninsula, where most homes have gates and names like Lotus or Mon Plaisir, a room rate that's less than your monthly salary is a true bargain. Amazingly, this gorgeous Italianate villa with turquoise shutters, just steps from town and around the corner from the prettiest beach, is relatively reasonable, even with neighbors like Microsoft cofounder Paul Allen and former French prime minister Raymond Barre.

> Many guests have been coming here for years. "We've grown old together," says the longtime proprietor

Dating from 1878, the seaside mansion is encircled by a beautiful garden filled with bougainvillea and palm, orange, and lemon trees; its various patios and terraces look out on the bright blue bay, the cliffs of the coastline, and, in the distance, Monaco and the Italian Alps. The 18 rooms are simply furnished with modern furniture and the occasional family armoire, but many share the amazing view, and a few (Nos.

3, 16, and 18) have spacious balconies. The sea panorama from No. 10's large, curved terrace is spectacular. There's no restaurant at the hotel, but a breakfast of juice, croissants, and jam is served on the patio.

This unfussy villa, which is closed November through January, attracts more than its share of actors and writers looking for a relaxing retreat. Many of the guests are repeat visitors who have been coming here for years and years; some guests have been coming for decades. "We've grown old together," says longtime proprietor Yves Maître-henry. He can be found on the premises with his wife, Michèle Reverchon—whose family took over the place in 1945—along with their various children and grandchildren. ⓘ *Saint-Jean-Cap-Ferrat, 011-33/4-93-76-04-36, hotel-brisemarine.com, $182–$207.*

Right: Dining alfresco at the Brise Marine. Left: Twin palms. Following pages: The hotel's Mediterranean view, and owner Yves Maîtrehenry.

# Tahiti

It would have been more accurate to name this chapter French Polynesia, because the hotels are actually on three islands: Moorea, Huahine, and Tahiti, all of which are part of the country of French Polynesia. But the word *Tahiti* is just so outrageously evocative—of aquamarine water, lush greenery, and lovely people—that it was impossible to resist. And that's the way it should be. After all, giving in to temptation has pretty much been a theme of visitors' trips to Tahiti (sorry, French Polynesia) since the days of Captain Cook. Who knows—that might be why the entire South Pacific has such a reputation for romance.

# Pension Mauarii

The only decent place to stay on the southern end of the island of Huahine, Pension Mauarii proudly grooms a castaway vibe. Door handles are fashioned from branches, buffed tree trunks act as pillars, and tubby tikis keep guard in

the courtyard. The ocean-side cabins are raised on stilts; at high tide, the water rushes below them. Capped by thatched roofs that are rigged with flap doors in order to catch the breezes, the chalets are twice the size of their competitors—and some even have interior sleeping lofts. All have giant bathrooms done in cracked tile and inlaid coral. Honeymooners may find a fertility totem standing at attention.

The young owner, Vetea, entertains guests over meals like a surfer-boy version of *Fantasy Island*'s Mr. Roarke. He's respected on Huahine for transforming a once-tired pension into a handsome, full-service resort. Unlike anywhere else in this price range, the Mauarii aims to provide everything a visitor might need—which is convenient, since Fare, the island's only real town, is at least a half-hour drive away. There's an activities concierge who can arrange wakeboarding; kitesurfing; catamaran, motorboat, and scooter rentals; free kayaks; and so on. Snorkelers, meanwhile, will be in heaven swimming with the eagle rays in the crystal-clear water right off the white-sand beach.

> Snorkelers will be in heaven swimming with the eagle rays right off the hotel's white-sand beach

The hotel has a gourmet restaurant, unusual for the island, that serves three meals daily. The restaurant's prices might be a little more than they have to be, but the food's good. For your island edification, there are nightly lectures about Polynesian life. Note: Rooms at Pension Mauarii book up fairly far in advance. ❶ *Huahine, 011-689/68-8649, mauarii.com, room $75–$90, bungalow $100–$150.*

Left: Catamaran rentals at Pension Mauarii. Right: Beach bum heaven. Preceding pages: A guest room loft. Following pages: The pension's dining pavilion

# Punatea Village

Punatea Village counters the Tahitian norm in many ways. Its rooms are sheltered from the road; it faces bracing surf rather than a peaceful lagoon (alongside a large white-and-black-sand beach); and it's big enough for kids to roam around, with a swimming pool in a garden grove and a private waterfall nearby. The Village offers bicycles, basic snorkeling equipment, and kayaks to guests free of charge and also organizes half-day trips to Vaipoiri Cave (a popular picnic spot) and boat trips to the quiet Tautira coast.

**The young, attractive Bordes family built everything at Punatea Village from scratch three years ago**

The young, attractive Bordes family, who live on the property with a bunch of cats and dogs, built everything from scratch three years ago. The four simple beach bungalows—bed, sofa, porch, no kitchen—are spaced out for maximum privacy. As is often the case with family-owned properties in Tahiti, there are also a few smaller, cheaper motel-style rooms sharing a building set back from the sea, but they can't compare with the romance of renting a private hut.

A live-in cook prepares full dinners for $25 (look for the tuna steaks with vanilla sauce) in a pavilion beneath the palms. The tuna, mahimahi, shrimp, and occasional spiny lobster originate in Pueu, a fishing village close by. Ask ahead and a picnic basket of seasonal fruit, fresh salad, and water will be put together for an excursion.

Punatea Village is an hour's drive from Tahiti's capital, Papeete, and a 15-minute drive from Teahupoo Beach (the waves there are cherished by professional surfers). The center of Tahiti Iti, the old-time Polynesian peninsula on which Punatea Village is located, is within walking distance. Twenty minutes away by car, the Paul Gauguin Museum exhibits a number of the artist's sculptures, wood carvings, and engravings, and often shows major works on loan from other institutions. Adjacent to the museum is a botanical garden with tropical plants from all around the world—some of which are fragrant enough to make any visitor want to drop out and move to the island.
ⓘ *Afaahiti, Tahiti, 011-689/57-7100, punatea.com, room $55, bungalow $90.*

**Right: One of the four bungalows at Punatea Village. Left: The dining area. Following pages: Offshore at Punatea**

# La Baie de Nuarei

When you tell any male Moorean that you're staying at La Baie de Nuarei, the first thing he'll ask is if you've had the good fortune of ever seeing the owners' beautiful daughters. To the frustration of single men across the island, the Kindynis girls have spent years attending college in Europe, leaving French-born papa Tamagna and mama Tamara (who is a beauty herself) to pour their energies into their inn, which they're in the process of expanding, adding two more bungalows to the current three.

They've spared no expense. Liberally embellished with whimsy—full-size mermaid frescoes in the bathrooms, metal dolphin sculptures springing from

showerheads—this enclave of secluded wooden homes feels more like an artist's retreat than a pension. Each cottage comes with a fully equipped kitchen, television, and sitting area.

The gated property is on a clear, shallow lagoon a few feet from Moorea's most popular public beach, Temae—and it faces the same massive underwater coral garden fronted by the Sofitel la Ora, which charges $230 more a night.

The views of Tahiti are almost paralyzing. Guests who manage to break the spell, however, can borrow boats and books, and there's always the option of indulging in a treatment at the best-equipped spa outside the big resorts, operated by the Kindynises as a sideline.

It's a 10-minute drive to the excellent restaurants at Cook's Bay. As for entertainment, Theater Village holds dance shows (featuring 60 performers in a natural setting), and airplanes and helicopters can provide a thrilling overview of the area. If that's not in the budget, ride the Little Train of Moorea—actually a truck made to look like a train—which stops at popular sights. ℹ️ *Maharepa, Moorea, 011-689/56-1563, labaiedenuarei.pf, from $154.*

Right: The view from La Baie de Nuarei. Left: A guest bathroom. Following pages: A bungalow kitchen, and a boat afloat at the hotel

# Hiti Moana Villa

Tahiti's sea-facing hotels all have the same noisy defect: They're on the busy main road, which hustles along the prime coastline and ruins the serenity. Hiti Moana Villa, on the southwest coast 40 minutes from Papeete, feels mostly removed from the hubbub because of its position on a large lagoon. The Brotherson family runs the establishment with exactitude. Son Steve keeps the 10-year-old property looking no older than two; mom Henriette, in her flowered dresses, tends the verdant courtyard gardens and koi pond.

Three garden bungalows, done in polished wood and vibrant colors, are within earshot of the morning traffic, but they come with furnished porches suited to sundowners and journal writing. Upgrading to one of the four ocean-facing bun-

galows near the pool and the boat ramp yields a quieter space with a kitchen and picture-window views of the lagoon—which, many days, is used for training by rowing teams in canoes.

Surfers and golfers will be thrilled by the location; one of Tahiti's best surf breaks (Papara, a black-sand beach) is nearby, as is Atimaono Golf Course, an internationally rated 18-hole facility (the only one on the island). The hotel's private boat is available for light fishing in the lagoon, and great snorkeling can be done off the coral reef. Nature buffs will find their entertainment hiking in the lush hilly interior.

For simple, no-nonsense meals, a handful of *roulottes*—evening-only food stands where you can get dinner for about $9—are a quick stroll away. You won't want to leave the islands of French Polynesia without trying a bowl of cold *poisson cru*. The traditional raw-fish dish captures the taste of the tropics, thanks to a dose of fresh coconut milk. ❶ *Papara, Tahiti, 011-689/57-9393, papeete.com/moanavilla, bungalow from $85, with kitchen from $115.*

Right: Hillside Hiti Moana Villa. Left: A bungalow. Following pages: Hiti Moana's patio and koi pond

# Fare Arana

Patrice Coucuret ran a popular bed-and-breakfast in Provence for more than 10 years. In 2002, tired of unexpected midnight appearances by weary road-trippers, Patrice; his wife, Nathalie; and their poodles decamped to a hillside in southwest Moorea. They wanted to be someplace where their guests would arrive announced and excited.

At first glance, Fare Arana is *très tahitienne*: Each guest gets a furnished patio and deck overlooking a lagoon, with the fragrance of flowers all about. But Patrice also brought the French bonhomie and pastis cocktails with him, which he uses to fuel conversations in a poolside cabana.

The name should have been the first clue: In some parts of French Polynesia, arana means "nest"

Faraway Provence, precious and countrified, fills the rooms. The bungalows have trim painted in periwinkle and cinnamon, wood-and-wicker decor tastefully accented with dried flowers, crockery-stocked kitchens with lace curtains and sea views, and—most unusual for these parts—air-conditioning.

The pool, dining, and sundeck areas are equally smart, with a daybed under a thatched roof, a lacy hammock, and wrought-iron tables and chairs with bold and beautiful floral-print tablecloths and cushions. The effect is adorable. Fare Arana's name should have been the first clue: In some parts of French Polynesia, *arana* means "nest."

For any guests who'd prefer to leave the planning to someone else, Fare Arana offers two-day and four-day packages that include not only accommodations but also island tours by boat or four-wheel drive and a visit to Tiki Village for the lively evening show. ℹ *Atiha, Moorea, 011-689/56-4403, farearana.com, from $140.*

Left: The deck and pool at Fare Arana. Right: Hanging out in a hotel hammock

# Acknowledgments

It takes a lot of great people to put together a beautiful book, and we give our hearty thanks to everyone involved.

First, there are the writers: Margie Rynn (Provence, French Riviera); Reid Bramblett (Tuscany, Jamaica); Ted Loos (Costa Rica); Brian Keeley (Bali); Jennifer Howze (Cornwall); Jason Cochran (Tahiti); David LaHuta (St. Lucia); Shana Liebman (Vieques); and Laurie Walsh-Kuntz (Bahamas). Jennifer Divina, Naomi Lindt, Melissa Denchak, and Suzy Walrath contributed additional reporting and editing. Tom Berger copyedited the book.

The photographs, edited by Amy Lundeen with assistance from Rebecca Simpson and Lauren Keenan, are by Galilea Nin (Provence, French Riviera); Greg Miller (Tuscany); Diane Cook and Len Jenshel (Tahiti); Thayer Allyson Gowdy (Costa Rica); Sue Parkhill (Cornwall); Amanda Marsalis (Bali); Emily Nathan (Vieques); Stewart Ferebee (Rockhouse Hotel and Country Country, Jamaica); Reid Bramblett (Jake's, Jamaica); Laurie Walsh-Kuntz (Seascape Inn, Bahamas); Image State/Alamy (Exumas, Bahamas); Comstock Images/Alamy (Andros Island, Bahamas); David LaHuta (Villa Beach, St. Lucia) and Luca Trovato/Getty Images (St. Lucia).

The design is by Pegi Goodman, Toby Fox, and Wilbert G. Gutiérrez.

Our thanks also go out to Kristen Latta, Leslie Stoker, Galen Smith, Liam Flanagan, Michael Jacobs, and the many other talented folks at Stewart, Tabori & Chang and Harry N. Abrams; our publishing consultant, Bruce Harris; and our lawyer, Randy Shapiro.

Hôtel Brise Marine, on the French Riviera. Following pages: Le Cadran Solaire, Provence

Finally, we're grateful to the
hoteliers, without whom
*Secret Hotels* could never exist

All information was accurate at time of printing. If you find something
has changed, please let us know at Letters@BudgetTravel.com.
For more smart travel advice, please visit us at BudgetTravel.com.

Published in 2007 by Stewart, Tabori & Chang
An imprint of Harry N. Abrams, Inc.

Library of Congress Cataloging-in-Publication Data:

Secret hotels / edited by Erik Torkells and the editors of Budget Travel magazine.
          p. cm.
ISBN-13: 978-1-58479-623-7
ISBN-10: 1-58479-623-5
1.        Hotels—Guidebooks.  I. Torkells, Erik.  II. Budget Travel.

TX907.S3895 2007
910.46—dc22

                                                        2007061726

Editor: Kristen Latta
Designers: Pegi Goodman, Toby Fox, and Wilbert G. Gutiérrez
Front cover design: Galen Smith and Budget Travel
Production Manager: Tina Cameron

The text of this book was composed in Gotham.

Printed and bound in China.
10 9 8 7 6 5 4 3 2 1

**HNA**
harry n. abrams, inc.
a subsidiary of La Martinière Groupe

115 West 18th Street
New York, NY 10011
www.hnabooks.com